Peace, Love, & Subs™

The True Cosmic Dave Story

Dave Lombardy

DB and MR Publications, LLC

Peace, Love, & Subs ™

The True Cosmic Dave Story

Cosmic Dave ™

Dave Lombardy

FIRST EDITION

Manufactured in the United States of America

Paperback ISBN: 979-8-9912083-0-7
eBook ISBN: 979-8-9912083-1-4
Hardcover ISBN: 979-8-9912083-2-1

Library of Congress Control Number: 2024915406

Note: In 2022, Dave's franchise company was sold to SRC DCS, LLC. Photos displayed before this time are designated "Historical pictures."

DB and MR Publications, LLC

Contents

Dedication

To my son, Brandon, and my daughter, Rachael.

And to my wife, Maryann, who, with her patience and
love, gave me the drive to never give up.

Chapter 1

The Hard Fall

I couldn't stop crying.

On some level it made sense. I'd lost my band, I'd lost my girl, I'd lost my dreams. I was twenty-nine and my life was effectively over. Of course, I'd be depressed. But the crying...it was endless. And if I wasn't crying, I felt like crying. I shouldn't have been *this* depressed. I didn't want to get out of bed, and I didn't care whether I lived or died. No, it was worse than that. I started to wish I was dead. Maybe then the fucking crying would stop.

Something—I don't know what—made me decide that I should get some help. I had the support of my parents—I always had the support of my parents—but I needed more. I couldn't go on like this. The problem was, I was so lost and confused that I didn't know where to look. I couldn't think; I couldn't reason. It was as if my mind had turned against me, and my thoughts were scattered everywhere. The only idea I could finally settle on was driving myself to the hospital. Maybe they'd know what to do.

At Hillcrest Hospital, a fifteen-minute drive from Mom and Dad's house in our Cleveland suburb, I walked in and told the woman at the front desk that I thought I was going to commit suicide. It was the only thing I could think of to say. Was I, really? I don't know. To this day, I don't know. I only know that I didn't care about living anymore.

They checked me into a room, asked me some questions, decided I might be serious about the suicide threat, and called my parents. I sat in a chair and considered where I was and suddenly everything seemed surreal to me. Nothing made any kind of sense. *How the fuck did I get here?*

Mere weeks before, I'd been in California, living the dream. Our band was going places. We'd played clubs in Los Angeles and San Francisco, clubs like the Starwood and Uncle Charlie's. We played with Steppenwolf, Huey Lewis, and Eddie Money. We watched Van Halen get their start. Carlos Santana was a neighbor of mine. So was Grace Slick. Sammy Hagar lived a few blocks away. Our band had a following. People loved us. I was recognized on the street and was even asked for my autograph. I was writing music, still looking for that breakout hit, but I knew it was coming. Any day now, we'd be hitting the big time. We were close to getting introduced to legendary promoter Bill Graham, owner of Fillmore Records. I had a girlfriend and a future I could only have ever dreamed of growing up in Beachwood, Ohio.

How did it all fall apart so fast?

My dad came into the hospital room and I started crying all over again. I told him I didn't want to live. I told him I had lost it all and I didn't know why. "What happened?" I said. "Where did it all go?"

Dad held me and said, "I'm proud of you, son. I'm proud of what you did out there. Your mother and I are both so proud."

And they were. They'd flown out to see me play. They'd even come out before the band, back when I was playing the role of Tony in *West Side Story*. Dad was part owner of a successful food wholesaling company. We lived well. Dad was a businessman, but he had an artistic side, and he appreciated my creative pursuits, seeing in me the road he hadn't taken but maybe wished he had. My success had been his success, too. Nobody had followed me closer.

"It's going to be okay, Dave," he said. "It's going to be okay."

I spent a couple of days at Hillcrest before the staff decided that a mental health facility would be a better fit and I was transferred. I spent two weeks at the facility, hanging out with the other patients, a group of unfortunate misfits that could all have played extras in *One Flew Over the Cuckoo's Nest*, while the nurses came around speaking in soft, patronizing tones, seemingly afraid that one sharp word might send us all over the edge. It never stopped seeming like some bizarre nightmare. One day I'm playing the Whisky, one day I'm in a mental institution.

Dad came every day. Mom came at least every other day. In the meantime, I had a complete physical and psychological exam. At one point, Dr. Wolf, the psychiatrist who had been evaluating me, came into my room when Dad was there to tell us of his findings. "Mr. Lombardy," he said to Dad, "your son has bipolar disorder. He's currently suffering from a manic-depressive episode." I had never heard of bipolar disorder. Neither had Dad, but we would learn that my manic episodes—extreme emotional swings—could go both up and down. And when they go down, they go *way* down. The depressive episode of someone living with bipolar disorder is exceedingly more intense than normal depression.

The explanation didn't help. So it had a fucking name. So what?

Dr. Wolf prescribed lithium, a drug designed to even out the mood swings. It seemed to help, but I had to stay at the mental health facility until they could establish that I could handle the drug without any serious side effects. A few days later, I was released to my parents' care.

Now I was back in my childhood home, soon working once again at my father's company. California was a dream from a million years ago. The lithium was effective in that I didn't wish I was dead anymore, but I also didn't feel much like living. I was just sort of in a stagnant emotional limbo, and two questions continued to rattle through my tortured mind. How in the fuck did I fall so hard, and how in the fuck was I ever going to get back up?

Chapter 2

Rock and Roll

Dad was a good-looking guy, with charm, an easy-going manner, and a great sense of humor, always putting me in mind of Dean Martin. I was named after his father, my grandfather—David Lombardy. Grandpa owned and operated one of the largest food wholesaling companies in the greater Cleveland area. But he died of cancer at the age of only forty-two, leaving my dad fatherless at sixteen.

Dad and his brother Ross and sister Marie inherited the business. In time, the Lombardy's joined forces with three other families to form Seaway Foods, an even larger company. With my two brothers and my sister, I enjoyed a very comfortable childhood. We lived in a beautiful house with a live-in maid in a wealthy neighborhood. Mom was a stay-at-home Italian mother, always cooking something. But she spent a lot of time on the golf course, too, eventually becoming good enough to turn pro. I was a happy kid and wanted for nothing.

As busy as Dad was with the business, he was a good family man, always making his best effort to be home every day by six o'clock, in time for dinner, and most days making it. He'd lie on his favorite couch in the evenings watching television and I'd be right there in the TV room with him, sitting on the carpet. I loved those evenings. Sometimes we'd watch movies together. I loved all kinds of movies, but I'd be sure to never miss anything with Marlon Brando in it. I wanted to be just like him, and I dreamed of someday being an actor. Dad understood. Dad was the artistic type, but the circumstances of his life put him forever in the business world.

I think Dad's artistic side drew him closer to me than to my siblings, something that caused resentment around the house. My siblings sensed the favoritism. It wasn't anything overt, but kids pick up on these things, and the resentment built and I don't think it ever really went away, even as we got older and became adults. For my part, I practically worshipped the man. We'd have Christmas parties at the house with a hundred or so people. I was outgoing and I'd mingle with the guests, and time and again, I'd hear, "You're just like your father!" In my mind, there was no better compliment.

I was popular at school, but I was a poor student. It wasn't as if I didn't try. But everything seemed hard to me. I'd find myself struggling with stuff that other kids picked up easily. I started at Gesu Catholic, but my parents eventually enrolled me in a Julie Billiart school for kids with learning disabilities. My siblings called me stupid and loser and made fun of me constantly. But I wasn't in Julie Billiart for more an a few weeks before it was decided that I should be attending public school. And so, it was Bryden Elementary and ultimately Beachwood High School.

All along the way, I hated it. School was just never for me. I hated the rules, the homework, the tests, everything. After I discovered girls, I at least had a reason to go. It was a largely Jewish school and I was Italian. With the girls, that gave me a sort of exotic magnetism. I was in demand. But other than the girls, there was nothing at school for me. Besides, why did I need school? What did I need to learn algebra and biology and history for? I was going to be an actor.

Or at least so I thought. But that idea changed dramatically on a February evening in 1964. Dad was on the couch and I was sitting on the floor as usual. We were watching the Ed Sullivan Show that night. Sullivan introduced a musical band that for some reason, I hadn't heard of before. But the crowd in the TV audience sure seemed to know who they were. They were going nuts. The guys were screaming and the girls were swooning. Four young men in suits with haircuts I would later come to learn were called "mop-tops" started playing, and my lifetime dream changed immediately. I sat there watching with my mouth hanging open. I was blown away. I no longer wanted to be an actor; I wanted to play rock and roll just like the Beatles, and there was nothing I was ever more certain of.

In typical fashion, Dad understood, and he did one better. He bought me a guitar. I practiced day and night in our basement and I got pretty good. And I listened to rock and roll constantly. Before the Beatles, I had heard the latest hits on the radio here and there, but now I was hooked on this new musical wave. I couldn't get enough of it. I dreamt of being a rock and roll star.

But something happened around that time that would derail my life for a year or so, and stay with me forever. I was fourteen. I'd hang out after school with a couple of buddies and every so often, there was an older guy, maybe twenty-one, who could come around. He played guitar and wore his hair in a long ducktail. I thought he was cool. One time, he invited me and a friend to his place near John Carroll University. What happened next, I can only remember in bits and pieces. He bragged about being able to hypnotize people and dared me to let him put me under. Whether he really did, I don't know, but I do remember him performing a sexual act on me. I don't recall anything else. I don't remember where my friend was, or even getting home, but I vividly recall being an emotional wreck for the next several days.

I felt shame. I felt like hiding. I tried to push the incident from my mind, but I couldn't let go of it. It was stuck in my head and there was no moving on from it. Finally, I walked into my parents' bedroom one morning while Dad was getting ready for work, and I broke down and told them what had happened.

Mom said, "I *knew* something was wrong. You've been so quiet!" Dad asked me about the guy who'd molested me, and I could see the anger in his eyes. He was losing it. I said I didn't know who he was, and I really didn't. He'd just been some guy that had started hanging out with us. Looking back, I'm sure he probably had us, or at least me, in his sights all along. But had he been in the room that morning, I'm sure my dad would have fucking killed him.

Dad hugged me as I cried and said, in words that would be repeated years later, "It's going to be okay, Dave. It's going to be okay."

Dad didn't go to work that morning. He and Mom sat with me and we talked for hours. It helped. But recognizing that I needed to better process what had happened to me, Dad called a mental counselor. It was the right idea. Other parents might have suggested I just "try to forget it" and move on, but my parents understood that that would have been impossible.

I would see the counselor for more than a year. Dad was involved the whole time and if we were close before, we became even closer after that. (Which, of course, sowed even more resentment from my brothers and sister.) As for the guy with the ducktail, I never saw or heard from him again.

There was something else in those days that helped me besides the counselor: the music. *Rock and roll.* I was still listening to it and still playing my guitar. In my sophomore year of high school, I found some bandmates, and we formed a group called "The Collection." We had two guitars, a bass, drums, and keyboards. I played guitar and was lead vocalist. We covered the Beatles, the Kinks, the Rolling Stones, and all the great groups of the time.

Three or four days a week, we'd practice in my basement. We sounded a little rough at first, but eventually, we started getting it together. And when we felt as if we'd practiced enough, we decided we were ready to start performing. Our first show was at our high school—Beachwood High, on a Friday night. Word went out through the school and 500 kids showed up to pack the auditorium. We were half excited and half nervous, but from the first note we played, they loved us. They cheered and applauded and yelled for more. I'd never experienced anything like it, never experienced the adulation of a crowd. It was intoxicating. The whole experience moved me, and from that moment on, I knew exactly where I wanted to be, exactly where I belonged—on stage, performing.

We started playing at the school every week. I was sixteen by then and I became even more popular with the girls. Italian *and* a rock star. At least at Beachwood. The guys loved us, too. Strangers came up to me in the hallways between classes to say, "Man, you guys are fucking great!" Everyone knew who we were. Before long, we were performing all over—other schools, churches, and some of the small colleges and universities in the area. We made a couple hundred bucks a gig, good money for teenagers back in those days. We were a bona fide professional rock and roll band. It was a blast being a local celebrity, and it was a blast playing rock and roll.

And of course, there was the partying. We were teenagers, after all. You wouldn't find us home on a weekend night, and a lot of times, not even on school nights. After concerts, we'd be out till all hours. Not far from my house was a 10,000-square-foot mansion, home to a young rich guy and his attractive wife. We'd party there from time to time, often until three or four in the morning. The husband would go to bed, but the wife continued to hang out with us, sometimes chasing us around the house.

School, meanwhile, continued to be a drag. I'd never warmed up to it, although I loved the social scene. Besides concerts and parties, there was always something going on. Basketball was huge and the games between Beachwood High and Shaker Heights were epic. But in class, I struggled. The teachers didn't seem to understand or help. There was one, Mr. Murano, who would punish a student for not paying attention by making the student stand with his nose pressed up against the brick wall of the classroom for the duration of the class. If you moved, he'd hit you.

He hit me one time when my parents happened to be in Florida. I mentioned it that evening to Uncle Lester, my dad's brother-in-law, who was staying with us while my parents were away. Uncle Lester was a wonderful man, a real Italian, and a builder by trade. He was loyal and protective, and he didn't take kindly to anyone messing with a member of the family. He went to the school the next day to talk to Mr. Murano, and Mr. Murano never bothered me again. I asked Uncle Lester one day what he'd said to Mr. Murano. "I said if he ever gave you a hard time again, I was going to use his head for a bowling ball." I have no doubt that Uncle Lester would have done so. Mr. Murano sure believed him.

Outside of class, the days and nights were special. It was all a part of being in a band, of being young and popular. And before long, I had a chance to become even bigger. A guy by the name of Eric Carmen lived close by. Eric played music, too. In fact, he'd been classically trained on the piano, but he taught himself the guitar after seeing the Beatles, just like me, and turned to rock and roll. I often wonder how many people were influenced by that Ed Sullivan performance. It seems as if a whole generation of musicians got their start wanting to emulate John, Paul, George, or Ringo.

Eric played in a few different bands and was forming a new one. I got the chance to audition. I did well, but Eric was well above my skill level at the time, and so were the guys that he eventually formed the band with, a group that called themselves the Raspberries. They'd go on to have big hits like "Let's Pretend" and the million-selling single "Go All the Way." Ultimately, Eric would have a successful solo career, releasing the classic "All by Myself" in the mid-seventies. Other hits would include "Never Gonna Fall in Love Again" and "Hungry Eyes."

I met Joe Walsh back then, too, a guy who would go on to become a rock and roll legend. Joe would make it really big with the Eagles just a few years later. He was a student at Kent State, and he played around the Cleveland area in a band called the James Gang. These guys would go on to record some classic rock tunes like "Funk #49" and "Walk Away." We were given the chance to open up for them a couple of times, once at St. Paschal's church in Highland Heights. What a thrill.

You could tell Joe was going to be great. The Kent State shooting happened while he was enrolled there, and soon afterward, he decided he didn't need college. He dropped out and played music full-time from that point on. I don't imagine he ever felt as if dropping out did him any harm.

Years after the Eagles, Joe Walsh's career would be managed by a friend of mine, David Spero. David got his start working for his father, Herman, producer of *The Upbeat Show*, a local music variety program that was ultimately syndicated and broadcast nationally. *The Upbeat Show* featured seemingly everybody at one time or another——James Brown; Frankie Valli and the Four Seasons; Blood, Sweat, and Tears, The Yardbirds; Stevie Wonder; The 5th Dimension; you name it. Eventually, David went on to become a DJ, and then a manager. He managed the Michael Stanley Band, a great example of a band that produced "heartland" rock, the simple, bluesy sound that Cleveland became known for. David managed to get Michael Stanley to open for the Eagles on one of their early tours, and that's how he came to know Joe Walsh.

Meanwhile, we kept playing. At home, Dad continued to be my biggest supporter, always keeping up with the latest goings-on of my life. He'd wait up for me when I'd come home late and we'd have long talks about anything and everything. He'd ask if I was hungry, and we'd make these great homemade sandwiches together. Being in the food business, Dad knew his stuff. The refrigerator was always full of the best meats and cheeses and sauces, most of it from Alesci's, an amazing Italian deli not far from us. We had the best breads, and we'd pile the sandwiches high and top them with fresh peppers and juicy slices of tomatoes, and eat them over the sink. We'd make different kinds, mixing the meats and cheeses and making new creations all the time.

How could I have known at the time what part those sandwiches would one day play in my life?

In the meantime, my social life continued to roll along. I was young and life held nothing but wonderous possibilities. With my popularity, I was meeting new people and hanging around with a different crowd. I lost track of some of my older friends, but life was good. Or so I thought. But before long, there was some friction in the band. We just didn't seem to be connecting the way we did before and we started playing less. Then one night, I was riding in a car with a friend from school and he turned to me and said, "Hey, you want to smoke some weed?" I'd never smoked weed before, but I was sure as hell willing to try it. Drugs were becoming part of the rock and roll world. Weed was cool, and I was cool. It sure seemed like the right thing at the time.

Chapter 3

The Hippy Life

From the first toke, I was hooked. I loved weed. It was mind-altering and relaxing at the same time. An anxious mindset would turn to a euphoric one. Before long, I was getting stoned every day after school. It became a part of my life, a big part. Not very long after I started smoking weed, I tried something else: LSD. Acid trips were even more far out, even more mind-altering. I loved the way it freed up my mind. Drugs were everywhere back in those days, and it wasn't hard to find whatever it was you wanted.

The guys in the band were getting stoned too. We'd get together to practice, but we'd spend the time just getting high. It showed. We lost our motivation. Soon, we were doing fewer concerts. And weed was beginning to affect other parts of my life. I hung around a different crowd now. I was becoming friends with the potheads, and my popularity as the Italian rocker started to fade.

At home, our live-on maid had moved out when we kids all started getting older, and her room, on the opposite side of the house from the other bedrooms, was now empty. I took it and spent my time holed up there, apart from the family, enjoying what felt like more independence. I listened to records constantly. I painted the room psychedelic colors and hung posters of rock and roll musicians—the Beatles, the Rolling Stones, the Kinks, and the band that was quickly becoming my favorite, the Moody Blues. I'd play their album *Days of Future Past* over and over, listening to "Tuesday Afternoon" and "Nights in White Satin." Their music was hypnotic.

Years later, I would think about how I decorated that maid's room. The colors, the posters, the rock and roll theme. Without my conscious effort to do so, it would be a motif that I would later recreate in a way I could never have imagined at the time.

I smoked weed in my new room. It went along with the psychedelic colors and the music. Mom and Dad suspected something, but they stayed away. In truth, they didn't know what to make of me. I was becoming distant, almost reclusive. Of course, my siblings disrespected me even more. They knew what was going on. First, they thought I was a stupid loser, and now they thought I was also a druggie. And they weren't shy about letting me know how they felt about me. Even if they didn't say anything to me directly, I could tell by their expressions when I'd come into a room.

Time went on. I kept smoking dope, doing acid, listening to music, and hating school. At home, I became even more aloof. Sometimes days would go by without my family even seeing me. I'd stay in my room, sneaking down to the kitchen to grab something out of the fridge to eat from time to time, and then retreating back to the room again. All the closeness I'd had with my parents, especially my dad, seemed to be gone. I didn't care, and I really had no idea of what my attitude was doing to them. They saw me as a surly teen. I'd changed. Looking back, especially as a father myself, I know it must have been difficult for them. At the time, all I knew was that they just didn't understand me.

One night, I came home late after partying at a friend's house to see the light on in my room. I was sure I'd turned it off. I always had. I'd turn off the light and close the door, signaling to everyone else in the house that my room was off-limits. But when I opened the door, there was my mother, going through my things. She was holding a bag of weed she'd found.

"Mom!" I said, "What are you doing in my room?"

"What's this?!" she demanded to know, waving the baggie.

"How come you're going through my stuff?!"

"Why are you doing drugs?" Mom said. She must have known I'd been smoking weed, but seeing the actual evidence was more than she could take. "How come you're doing this to us?" she cried.

Things got worse from there. We shouted over each other, neither one even listening to the other. The shouting got even louder until I finally yelled, "You know what? Fuck this! I'm out of here!"

I stormed out of my room and downstairs where Dad was standing, having heard the whole thing. Then I began arguing with him. More shouting. More yelling. Finally, I blurted out, "*Fuck off!*"

The arguing stopped. Dad raised his hand and slapped me so hard I fell to the floor. I looked up to see Mom standing there in disbelief, blinking away tears. Dad looked as if he'd surprised himself with the slap, but he also looked like he might be ready to deliver another one. Nobody said a word and the room got deathly quiet. After several seconds, I picked myself up and ran out of the house, jumped into my car, and drove off into the night.

It wasn't as if I didn't have anywhere to go. My friend Timmy had left his parents' house several months earlier and had a little apartment in Coventry Village, about twenty minutes away. He was looking for a roommate and had mentioned the place to me a few different times. I kept telling him I'd think about it. I hadn't been ready to move out of my parents' house, but now it looked as if I didn't have a choice. Timmy had his roommate.

—◦—

San Francisco had its Haight-Ashbury, New York City had its Greenwich Village, and Cleveland had its Coventry. What was once a charming mostly Jewish community became, by the late 1960s, a thriving counterculture scene. Coventry Village was all bars and record stores and head shops. There was a trendy clothing shop that was reportedly visited by John Lennon and Paul McCartney when the Beatles played at Cleveland Municipal Stadium on August 14, 1966, part of their final tour. Record Revolution, now a legendary record store had just opened there, too, and rock stars used to visit it for album signings when they were in town. Coventry was the place to be. It was like a continuous pop festival. There were people everywhere, and everyone was happy and cool and hip. Rock and roll played in the streets, the smells of marijuana and incense hung in the air, and hippies wearing bell bottoms, and beads, and flowers in their hair hung out on every corner. Sex was easy and drugs were omnipresent. People walked around smoking joints, and the cops always looked the other way.

I felt right at home.

The circumstances of my being there were unfortunate. I didn't like being estranged from my family. I missed my parents. I missed the comforts of our upper-middle-class house. On the other hand, the Sixties were in full swing and in retrospect, there's nowhere I'd have rather been. These were some of the best times of my life.

It's hard to describe the Sixties to anyone who hadn't lived them. So much was going on at once. The Vietnam War was raging. I knew guys who'd been drafted. I probably would have been drafted myself if the war had continued another year or so. At the time, I was still in high school. Technically, at least. Living in Coventry, I didn't exactly attend Beachwood High on a regular basis. Where I was living, anti-war sentiment was strong.

There were demonstrations everywhere. "Stop the War" was spray-painted onto buildings. Kent State was just an hour south of us and when the National Guard opened fire on the crowd of protesting students, killing four of them, that was all anybody talked about. The news coverage of it was constant; every time you turned on the radio or TV, there was another report about the shooting and its aftermath. It seemed the country was mostly starting to turn against the war, but we were in too deep and it continued to drag on and on.

The civil rights movement was strong too. Riots erupted in cities across America. In the Hough district of Cleveland, riots broke out in July of 1966 and the mayor called in the National Guard. There were similar scenes all over the country. Martin Luther King, Jr. was assassinated in Memphis in 1968. Bobby Kennedy was assassinated in Chicago the same year. Richard Nixon got elected president after Lyndon Johnson decided not to run for a second term. He'd had enough. The times were crazy.

And underlying it all was rock and roll. By the mid-60s, the Beatles had transformed themselves from their "I Want to Hold Your Hand" music to their Sgt. Pepper stuff, and the music world followed them. Bob Dylan went electric, melding folk music with rock, and suddenly lyrics mattered. The Byrds, the Who, Jimi Hendrix, Janis Joplin, Joni Mitchell, Crosby Stills Nash and Young, the Grateful Dead, Jefferson Airplane, Cream, Credence Clearwater Revival, and about a thousand other great artists and bands were making amazing music, inspiring and influencing each other to spawn a creative period of sound the world had never seen. It seemed that something completely new and incredible was being released every day by somebody. And I was soaking all of it in.

I grew my hair long and became a full-fledged hippie and loved every minute of it. I even went to Woodstock in 1969, the defining 1960s event. Except that we didn't quite make it. With six other guys in a van, I rode the nine hours to Max Yasgur's farm in New York, but we got bogged down in the lines of traffic. Nobody expected all the people that showed up. Organizers of the "Three Days of Peace and Music" festival expected somewhere around 50,000 attendees. Almost ten times that many came. Almost half a million. It was pure insanity. On top of that, I did three tabs of acid along the way. I never made it out of the van.

The drugs actually became a problem. Some of the guys around me started doing heroin. Nobody really knew the dangers back then. Nobody knew how addictive it was. Drugs were just becoming part of the culture. Me, I stayed away from heroin only because I was deathly afraid of needles. Otherwise, I have no doubt I'd have tried it. Who knows where that might have led? I know this much: eventually, I would lose four friends to heroin overdoses.

I did other stupid things back then. I was at a friend's house one night and there was a gun in the house. I grabbed it and put it to my head, just to show what kind of balls I had. Or at least I imagine that was the idea. Whatever was going through my mind, I pulled the trigger, assuming the gun wasn't loaded. The gun didn't go off, but then I pointed it at the window and pulled the trigger. And promptly shot out the window. I stood there for a second unable to move, then my legs went weak and I sank to the floor where I sat for quite some time. That episode still scares the shit out of me.

But overall, I was enjoying the days and nights of Coventry Village. I also kept missing my parents, however. There was a big hole in my life, and no amount of drugs or music or hippie life could fill it. My parents missed me, too, and worried about me. But nobody on either side was going to budge; nobody wanted to be the first to cave. Then came Uncle Lester to the rescue.

Uncle Lester and my dad had become close friends over the years. He was close to me, too, and it broke his heart that we we'd had such a huge fight and that I'd left. He couldn't allow himself to remain uninvolved. So, without any prompting from either side, Uncle Lester came to my place one evening to convince me to come home.

I had him come in and we sat on the couch in Timmy's living room.

"Your parents are worried about you, Dave," he said. "They want you home." Then he looked around at the cramped apartment, the shabby furniture, the cheesy hippy décor. "Don't you want to come home?"

"There are too many differences, Uncle Lester," I said. "I like it here. I have freedom. I can come and go as I please and do what I want. Mom and Dad don't understand me."

"Dave, I think you're underestimating them. They're understanding people and they love you dearly. And your dad's one of the greatest guys I know. You're forgetting how much you two have in common."

He was right about that, of course.

"When I see you," Uncle Lester continued, "I see your dad."

"I guess so." Actually, Uncle Lester had told me that before. And maybe that's why he'd been so great to me over the years. I had always felt close to Uncle Lester and his wife, Marie. I loved it when we visited with them, and I always looked forward to whenever they'd come over. And when we had family get-togethers, or Dad and Mom would throw a holiday party, I would end up sitting with them, talking and laughing with them all evening.

"Let's at least go talk to your folks," Uncle Lester continued. "You've got nothing to lose by doing that, right? Come on, Dave. What do you say? Let's go home, okay?"

I was ready, more so than I realized. Uncle Lester made me see how much. I'd been gone six months, and I wanted to be back with Dad and Mom. I was still just a kid, after all. Maybe I didn't know it at the time, but I had not outgrown my parents. Not by a long shot. I packed up the few things I had and told Timmy how much I appreciated staying with him. Then I went with Uncle Lester.

We drove home and I could feel my heart beating faster the closer we got. Everyone was there when we arrived. Mom started to cry, and I wanted to hug her.

But then Dad said the worst thing he could have said: "I knew you'd be back."

However I felt about coming home, the mood was totally broken. "Okay, that's it," I said, turning to leave. "I'm out of here!"

Uncle Lester grabbed me and then turned to Dad. "Chuck," he said, "your son came home because he wanted to try to work things out. Can't you see that? Now, look, you've got to fix this. You guys love each other too much for this to go on."

I broke free and headed for the door.

Behind me, I heard my dad. "Stop," he said.

I turned toward him. His expression softened. "I...I don't want you to leave," he said. "Damn it, Dave, stay here. With your family."

"But...but we're not going to get along," I said. "It won't be any different."

"Dave," Uncle Lester said, "Your family wants you home. Isn't it obvious? You guys can work this out, I know you can." Then his eyes went from me to Dad to Mom. "For the love of God, can we start acting like a family and put all this behind us?"

Dad hesitated for a moment, and then he strode over to me and put his arms around me and squeezed me tight. I squeezed right back and said I was sorry. He said the same.

"I love you, Dad," I said.

"I love you too, son," Dad replied. Then Mom hugged me. Then Uncle Lester hugged Dad. Everyone was hugging everyone and we were all crying. Everyone besides my siblings. My older sister gave me the coldest stare I'd ever seen and my older brother looked like he wanted to kill me. But I didn't care. Everything was all right again with my parents and me. Coventry had been a blast and I wasn't going to stop being a hippy, maybe ever, but I was home now, and that's where I belonged.

Chapter 4

California Dreamin'

I stopped the drugs after I moved back home. Looking back, I don't know that I would have stopped if I had stayed with Timmy. Uncle Lester might well have saved my life. There would be other angels in my life, three very important ones in my ultimate career, but Uncle Lester would always be the original angel. A lifesaving angel.

In addition to stopping the drugs, I cut my hair, too, at least a little. And I returned to school on a regular basis. Somehow, I even managed to graduate. Graduation turned out to be a blast. Everyone was celebrating and laughing, and it was fun reminiscing with people about our high school years. Everybody remembered me from before I was getting stoned all the time and missing classes. I kept hearing, "Dave, I'll never forget The Collection. You guys were great!" and "Dave, remember that time—," and then they'd launch into some funny story. It was a joyful evening and it made me grateful for all the wonderful moments I'd experienced at Beachwood High and all the great friends I'd met. It was fun looking back at it all. Maybe I hadn't been the best student, but I sure made a lot of special memories.

And I was at least a good enough student to get accepted into college. On family vacations to Florida, I'd noticed Miami Dade College in Miami. It was pretty much expected by my parents that I'd get a university degree somewhere. I was lukewarm on the idea, but figured if I was going to go, why not get away from home and head to the Sunshine State? I liked the idea of being more independent, and I liked the idea of spending the winter months away from the cold and gray of Cleveland. I had no clue what I was going to study. For some reason, law was in the back of my mind, even though I couldn't imagine being an attorney. I guess I just needed to pick something, and that seemed as good as anything.

I arrived at Miami Dade in the summer of 1970, a couple of months before classes started. Mom and Dad came down with me, then dropped me off at the apartment complex near campus that I would now be calling home. I stood outside of it as they drove off, feeling a little unmoored, realizing I was now a long way from home, and wondering if I'd made the right decision. Maybe I wasn't ready for the independence I had sought. Maybe I should have picked a school closer to the people who loved me. I walked in about the same time another new student was walking in, a really attractive girl named Mary Jane. We talked a bit and I felt a connection. Suddenly being away from home didn't seem so bad.

Until school started, I hung out in my small apartment, made some friends, smoked a little weed, saw Mary Jane, and went to some concerts. Life in Florida was going to be all right. Deciding to fly home for the Fourth of July, I boarded a plane that went first to Atlanta before continuing on to Cleveland. What I didn't know when I boarded was that Atlanta was about to host the second Atlanta International Pop Festival. The first was in 1969, about a month before Woodstock. About 150,000 people attended the festival to see a lineup that included Led Zeppelin, Creedence Clearwater Revival, Chicago, Janis Joplin, Canned Heat, and a bunch of other great rock and roll artists. It was such a success, that they had decided to do it again.

This year, they had an equally solid lineup planned. On the plane, I learned about the Festival and also learned that Jethro Tull was going to play there. So were the bands Ten Years After and Mountain. How did I learn all this? Because Jethro Tull, Ten Years After, and Mountain were *on my plane.* I couldn't believe it. And I was right in the midst of them. Ian Anderson, lead singer for Jethro Tull, sat right next to me! These guys had all come from other places where they had been touring and for some reason decided to party in Miami for a couple of days before flying up to Atlanta. Now they were all together heading for another wild music festival.

It was the craziest plane ride of all times—the best flight I've ever been on, before or since. Ian Anderson was hilarious. All the guys in the band were joking and laughing. I felt like I was on the personal private jet of all these wonderful musicians. Not long after takeoff, someone started passing a joint around. These were the days when you could still smoke cigarettes on a plane, but that didn't mean you could smoke dope. I thought the flight attendant was going to have a stroke.

"You...you can't do that!" she stammered.

"We can do anything," one of the guys said. "We're rock stars!"

I looked around our section and everyone was laughing their asses off. All the passengers enjoyed the flight. Drinks were ordered, funny stories were told, and everyone had a great time. It was a two-hour party, and the only time I've ever been sorry that a plane flight had to end. Needless to say, my plans changed. Fuck going to Cleveland. Cleveland could wait. I got off the plane in Atlanta with my new friends and headed for the Pop Festival.

I wasn't disappointed. The Festival ran from July 3 to July 5, and in addition to the guys on the plane, the schedule included Jimi Hendrix, the Allman Brothers, Mott the Hoople, It's a Beautiful Day, B.B. King, Johnny Winter, Grand Funk, and a dozen other great bands. For some reason, Jethro Tull never took the stage, but everybody else did.

The festival actually took place in Byron, Georgia, in a huge field, well south of Atlanta. The promoter expected about 100,000 people to show up, the same or a little less than the previous year's festival. Five times that many came. Some sources even said as many as 600,000. More than Woodstock. So many people flooded in that they gave up selling tickets. By the time I got there, it was free. With everyone else, I just walked right in.

Temperatures rose to 100 degrees, but nobody seemed to care. The whole place was drugs and fun-loving hippies. And the god of the moment was music—rock and roll. Quickly, the festival became known as "Woodstock of the South." Maybe I'd missed the original, but I didn't miss this one.

Hendrix was amazing. He played the *Star-Spangled Banner* on his guitar, just like he'd famously done at Woodstock. It was out of this world. Of course, no one could possibly have imagined that a couple of months later, Hendrix would be gone, dead of an overdose of barbiturates in London. Looking back, that made this performance all the more special to me.

By the time Jimi started playing the *Star-Spangled Banner*, I had worked my way closer to the stage. And like a lot of the festival-goers, I didn't come unprepared. I had a baggie with a couple dozen hits of acid in it. I passed it around and everyone in my area was soon tripping like crazy. At one point, I turned around, and right behind me in the crowd was a guy that I swear to this day was Dustin Hoffman. I can't prove it, but if it wasn't Dustin Hoffman, it was a dead ringer for him.

Meanwhile, I met a beautiful girl at the festival and we ended up being together for most of it. She lived in Atlanta, and after the festival finally ended, we went to her apartment. I was dumbfounded to see that she didn't own a single stick of furniture, save for her bed. No couch, no chairs, no tables. Instead, there were books everywhere. Stacks of them. And the only thing on the walls was a solitary poster of Jim Morrison in her bedroom.

And then things got weirder. "Dave," she said, "I should tell you something about myself."

"What's that?"

"I'm a witch."

"You're a witch?"

"Yes, a witch." She claimed she could tell me all about myself. And in fact, she said some things that were eerily close. She knew some stuff about me that even people close to me hadn't known.

I stuck around for a day or so, but then it was time to get back to Miami. Several years later, just to see how this chick was doing, I called her up. I swear, before I could even get a word out, she said, "Dave, I knew you'd be calling." Who knows, maybe she really was a witch.

Back at Miami Dade, classes finally started and I was reminded immediately how much I hated school. I guess I expected it to be somehow different than high school, but sitting in class certainly seemed the same—everyone frozen in their seats staring toward the front, taking down notes on what the guy up there was saying. The only difference was the size of the classes. My first class took place in a classroom the size of an auditorium. I listened to the professor drone on for twenty minutes and knew this shit wasn't for me. I left out the back door.

I'd go to classes occasionally, but mostly I'd party. I'd stay up late and sleep through the mornings. I was smoking weed pretty much every day and doing acid regularly, too. I was in Miami for a year and a buddy of mine calculated that in that time, we did 250 hits of LSD. That's a lot of acid. So, between the weed and the acid, and spending time with Mary Jane, whom I continued to see, I didn't exactly have a lot of time for school.

From time to time, I'd fly home to visit Mom and Dad for a long weekend. It was always good to come home and get caught up with them. I'd spend time seeing friends, too. On one of those trips home, a buddy of mine from high school stopped by. Rick was leaving the very next day for California. He had enrolled in Los Angeles Valley College, and he started talking excitedly about L.A. and about the school.

"Hey, come with me," he said. "I mean you and me in California? We'd have a blast." I got fired up listening to him. By that time, I'd already pretty much decided I was going to drop out of Miami Dade. There was nothing keeping me there, and I had no plans for whatever was going to come next. Why not go with Rick?

I ran inside the house. "Mom! Dad! I'm going to Los Angeles!"

True to form, Mom and Dad supported my decision and the next day, Rick and I lit out in my Datsun 240Z, two carefree hippies heading for the West Coast. It was exciting and life seemed full of possibilities again. Six days later, we arrived in Valley Glen in north Los Angeles. We found an apartment, signed a lease, and checked into the school.

Classes didn't start for a couple of weeks so we decided to see a little of Southern California in the meantime. We drove around Hollywood and Beverly Hills, and visited Santa Monica. One evening we drove up the coast and came upon Santa Barbara. It was after midnight when we arrived and as we cruised around the downtown area, we saw young people hanging out, listening to music, smoking weed. I liked the vibe. It reminded me a little of the Coventry. We parked and walked around. Santa Barbara looked beautiful, and the people were all cool.

"Rick," I said, "I don't want to go back to L.A . tonight. Let's hang here."

"Sure, but we're going to need a place to crash." Then he pointed to a record shop that was still open. "Let's ask in there."

The girl working in the shop was getting ready to close the store when we went in and I explained that we needed a place to sleep for the night. "We drove up from L.A.," I told her, "and we've decided to stay overnight. You know anywhere we can crash?"

She looked us up and down for a moment and I guess we didn't look like serial killers, so she said, "Sure. You can stay at my place."

That sounded great to us until the girl's boyfriend came in to pick her up and she explained that we were coming along. He got pissed and the two got into a pretty heated argument about it, finally settling down enough to suggest that we ask a cop. "The cops are really cool here," the girl said. "They can find you a place."

Back out in the street, we spotted a cop who knew where we might be welcomed. "Two blocks over," he said, and he gave us the address. "Lots of people come and go to that house. Kids, you know, about your age. I'm sure they'll let you stay."

The house was quiet when we got there. We knocked, didn't hear anybody, then pushed the unlocked door open. Inside, it was dimly lit but we could see a guy sitting at the kitchen table, eating something out of a can. There was a cat sitting on the table with him and the cat was eating too. Looking closer, we could see that the pair were eating the same meal: cat food. Rick and I looked at each other, and then I turned to the guy and said, "Um...we were told maybe we could crash here for the night?"

The guy didn't say a word. He just nodded slightly toward the darkened living room where there was a sofa and chair and went back to his Nine Lives.

Rick and I went into the living room, which, besides the sofa and chair, had nothing in it except stacks of books, reminding me a little of the witch's apartment in Atlanta. I got a little bit of a weird feeling, but it was only getting later and I really needed some sleep.

"You did the driving," Rick said. "Take the sofa. I'll sleep in the chair."

"Thanks," I said. "I need to go take a leak."

I hated to interrupt the cat dude, but I had to ask where the bathroom was. He pointed down the hall, still not saying anything, and I made my way toward the bathroom. In the semi-darkness, I could make out something moving on the carpet at the end of the hall a few feet from what I gathered was the bathroom door. I heard muffled, groaning voices, too. Somebody on the floor? As I got closer, I could see it wasn't one person, but two, a guy and a girl. And they were humping like crazy. *What the hell kind of house was this?*

I stopped in my tracks and considered going back to the living room, but I *really* had to go. The problem was that there wasn't enough room to get around the amorous couple. I hesitated for a moment, cleared my throat a little loudly so they'd know someone was present, and said, "Excuse me." Then I stepped over them, careful not to interrupt them or step on something important. I wasn't even sure they noticed.

No more than ten feet away from them, I was taking a piss when suddenly the girl, naked as naked gets, crawled into the bathroom and right up to me. Inches away from my penis, she looked up and said, "Hi."

"Hi," I replied.

"Where are you from?"

"Ohio," I managed to say, feeling my cheeks burning. "Cleveland."

"Cleveland," she repeated, now looking at my penis. "That's cool. So, what are you doing here?"

"Well, my buddy and I are enrolled in Los Angeles Valley College," I said. I stopped pissing. How could I piss with the girl staring at my dick? "We just drove up here for the day and we thought we'd stay over. We were told it would be okay to crash here for the night."

The girl nodded. "Sure. It's cool. Well, enjoy your stay." Then she crawled back to the guy in the hallway and the two started all over.

I was able to finish what I started and left the bathroom, stepping carefully over the couple again. I headed back to the living room and behind me, I heard the girl say, "Nice to meet you."

Back in the living room, I said, "Rick, you have *got* to go to the bathroom."

"I don't need to go."

"Trust me. You need to fucking go to the bathroom."

"Why?"

"Just fucking do it, okay? You won't be sorry, I promise."

Rick got more or less the same performance I got, and then we just sat in the living room laughing like hell.

"Santa Barbara, huh?" I said, trying to catch my breath.

"Fucking insane!" Rick said.

Neither one of us could stop laughing for the longest time. Then we tried to get some sleep. We didn't get much. Toward sunrise, people started coming into the house, maybe ten or fifteen, mostly guys, but a couple of girls. The place became a beehive of activity, with everyone talking in low voices and taking things out to a car that was parked outside. At one point, I noticed one of the guys had a gun.

"Rick," I whispered, "You awake?"

"Yeah."

"I think we ought to get out of here. Something doesn't feel right."

Rick nodded. "Yeah, this place is freaky. Let's bolt."

We slid out the front door, and then started walking toward where I'd parked the car. Along the way, I noticed a small diner, and Rick and I went in for some breakfast. It was a friendly little joint, and I asked around if anybody knew what the story was behind the house we'd just stayed in. That's when we found out the place was the local headquarters for Students for a Democratic Society.

Now, that in and of itself was interesting. I knew that the SDS was an activist organization, a leftist group with informal chapters of students at college campuses all across the country, as many as 300 chapters, in fact, by the end of the '60s. In 1962, the group had produced the famous Port Huron Statement, a manifesto calling for a more equal society and criticizing the capitalist status quo. But the idea that we stayed in their local HQ got a lot more interesting when we later heard about the Bank of America that was burned to the ground in Isla Vista, just off the campus of the University of California Santa Barbara.

It happened just a few short months after we were there. UCSB students stormed the building. This was after riots had broken out on campus over the Vietnam War. The day before, a civil rights activist by the name of William Kunstler—a lawyer who became famous for defending the "Chicago Seven," a group of radicals that had organized protests at the Chicago Democratic National Convention in 1968—had given an on-campus speech. Among other things, he said, "I have never thought that breaking windows and sporadic violence is a good tactic. But on the other hand, I cannot bring myself to become bitter and condemn young people who engage in it." According to those who were there, the students took this as permission to go a little crazy. Protests led to rock throwing, cops were called, the protests became riots, and then everything culminated in the storming of the bank building. The place was lit on fire, and with the rioting in full force, the fire department refused for safety reasons to enter the area, leaving the bank to burn to the ground.

Now, Rick and I could never be sure about the role of the SDS in the riot and burning of the bank, nor did we really want to know. All we knew was that the house we spent the night in weirded us out. Santa Barbara was a cool town and I was glad we stopped there, but on the morning we left, we were happy to be on the road again.

Chapter 5

Actor

Between Carmel and San Simeon, there's a rugged section of California called Big Sur. Rick and I discovered it after leaving Santa Barbara and heading north on Highway 1. The two-lane road hugged the winding coastline for a couple of hours until we found ourselves driving atop stunningly magnificent cliffs. At that point of the Central California coast, the Santa Lucia Mountains rise insanely out of the Pacific Ocean. You drive along, several hundred feet in the air, forest and mountain on one side of you, and, on the other side, the blue Pacific down below. It might be the most awesome stretch of scenery in the country. It was definitely the most awesome stretch Rick and I had ever seen. It almost didn't seem real.

I pulled the car over and we walked over to the guardrail at the edge of the road and looked down at the ocean. There was nothing but sheer cliff in front of us and I could feel my heart race. The wind was in my face, and way below, I could see humongous waves crashing into the shore. Beyond the horizon, the Pacific went on forever.

We crossed back over the road and started walking through the woods on the other side, deep and dense and otherworldly, a floor of pine needles under our feet and a cool forest breeze rustling the leaves and blowing through our hair. The trees seemed to grow all the way to the clouds.

Hiking trails, huge redwoods, and gorgeous, rocky beaches. Big Sur had it all. There were national parks, and campgrounds, and stretches of roadside shops and restaurants. And everywhere we looked, the scenery was spectacular. At the time Rick and I came upon this magical region, it had become a magnet for the hippies of the '60s. Kids from all over the country had come west, some, like us, heading for L.A., some heading for San Francisco, and many finding the counterculture they'd been looking for in between, in the beautiful backdrop of this enchanting piece of California. Hippies were camped out everywhere—in the woods, in the fields, on the beaches. Drugs were everywhere, too. The area attracted people from all over, and by then, there had been several folk festivals, with the likes of Crosby,

Stills, Nash, and Young; Joan Baez; Joni Mitchell; and the Beach Boys performing for the crowds that came. Big Sur was the perfect haven for the times.

Rick and I sensed it at once. Big Sur had the vibe of Haight-Ashbury and the scenery of Heaven. We drove around, and I could feel the area in my soul. It was spiritual. I felt like I belonged. I'd never seen anything like Big Sur, and yet in some way, it seemed familiar, like I'd always been there. I was completely enamored, and though we hadn't planned to, we stayed a few days. It was too awesome a place to spend just one day there.

On our last night, amid the beauty of Big Sur, we came upon a small concert in a field and listened to music and got high. We met some beautiful people and slept under the stars. The night was perfect. Driving back to Los Angeles the next day was depressing. How could we leave such an amazing place? It seemed to me as though God had intended people to be in places like Big Sur, places where you could live in awe of our creator, not in places like Los Angeles. All I could hope was that maybe someday I'd return.

On the way out of the area, I spotted a hitchhiker and we decided to pick him up. People did that back in those days without giving the idea a second thought.

My Datsun wasn't really made for a third passenger, but somehow, he managed to squeeze in.

"We're heading for L.A.," I said.

"That's cool. I'm just going a little ways. I'm Jim. Mind if I smoke a joint?"

"I'm Dave and this is Rick. Sure, do whatever you want, buddy."

We drove and Jim started smoking a joint and we talked about Big Sur and the folk music festivals.

"They're cool," Jim said. "And smaller and more laid-back than the big festivals. Like the Atlanta Pop Festival. Man, I was there last year and it was fucking huge. I mean, hundreds of thousands of people, you know?"

"You were there?" I said. "At the Atlanta Pop Festival? Man, *I* was there."

"No shit?"

"No shit."

"Man, it was crazy, wasn't it?"

To this day, I cannot believe what Jim said next.

"I was watching Jimi Hendricks," he continued, "and I swear, right next to me was Dustin Hoffman. Isn't that wild? Just rockin' out with everybody else. And then, some dude in front of me had a baggie full of acid and he was sharing it with everyone around! I was tripping all night. Man, it was insane!"

I just about drove off the cliff. "If you think that was insane," I said, "get a load of this: that dude with the acid? That was me!"

"No fucking way!"

We all just started laughing. It was mind-blowing. Two strangers who had been unknowingly together at one place had stumbled upon each other at another place 3,000 miles away.

We talked some more about music and concerts and finally, an hour or so south of Big Sur, Jim said, "This is good here, man. Thanks for the ride."

I pulled over and we said goodbye.

"Maybe I'll see you at the next music festival," Jim said.

"I'll bring the acid," I grinned.

Then it was back on the road to Los Angeles and the depression started kicking in again. The last few days had been fun and crazy. The cat dude, the couple having sex, hanging out in the headquarters of the SDS, the magic of Big Sur, the outdoor concert under the stars, and meeting Jim from the Atlanta Pop Festival—it was like some wonderful, crazy dream. Now it was back to the real world.

The day after we got back to our apartment was even more depressing. I went to my first class at Los Angeles Valley College. In a giant, semi-circular lecture hall filled with several hundred students, I listened for a half-hour as the professor rambled on and on. It was Miami-Dade all over again. I'm not sure why I expected anything different, but I'd just come from one of the most beautiful places on the planet, and here I was, held captive in a hardback chair in a cold, concrete building listening to some college instructor drone on about some subject I couldn't give a shit about. I walked out of the class and back to the apartment. I knew I wasn't going to return to school. There was no way. I stayed a few more months in Van Nuys, then called my parents to tell them I was coming home. Again.

Back home, I sat down with Dad. I told him everything. I told him all about California, about Santa Barbara, about Big Sur, about Valley College, and about how I couldn't stand to be in class.

"School's just not for me," I said. "I just can't do it."

Dad knew I was right. There was no use in trying to force me into being a student. I couldn't make it through a single class. How was I going to make it through four *years* of classes? But if I wasn't going to go to college, what was I going to do? We thought about it, and we both remembered my dream from when I was younger, my dream of being an actor. With The Collection, I had experience performing on the stage, but I didn't believe that rock and roll was my destiny. Acting was my destiny. Stage plays, musicals, movies. If I wasn't going to chase my dream now, when I was young, would I ever?

Somewhere along the way, I had learned about the American Academy of Dramatic Arts in Pasadena, California, a stone's throw from Hollywood. My future started there, and I was sure of it. I mentioned it to Dad. "Maybe that's where I should be," I told him. "Maybe my future is out there." I shouldn't have been surprised that he supported the idea. Of course, he would.

"But, listen, Dave," he told me. "Let's do it right. I want you to spend a year here first, working with me at Seaway Foods. Put some money away. Make sure you're ready. Then you can follow your dreams after that. Okay?"

Dad's condition sounded more than fair. Life had been a whirlwind anyway. I could use a year at home to regroup, save my money, and prepare for Pasadena. In the meantime, I signed up for classes at Fairmount Center for the Arts just outside of Cleveland not far from our house. I took dance classes, acting classes, even yoga classes. If I was going to follow my dream, I was going to do it right. I also got parts in some plays at nearby Chagrin Valley Little Theater, providing me with some valuable stage experience.

Eventually, I applied to the American Academy and was accepted pending an audition. As it happened, the Academy hosted auditions all over the country. They were coming to Cleveland, and I needed to get ready. I knew I had only one shot.

I prepared for the audition like Rocky Balboa prepared for his fight with Apollo Creed. I even worked out, getting up early and jogging every morning. I wanted to be fit, and ready for anything they'd throw at me. As the day of the auditions approached, I calmed my nerves by taking long, meditative walks in the woods. I'd visualize the audition, being up on stage in front of the American Academy representatives, all eyes on me.

Finally, the big day arrived. Auditions were held in a theater in downtown Cleveland. When my turn came, I felt a rush of adrenaline and excitement, but I knew I was ready. They started by asking me questions. "Why are you here" "Why do you want to be an actor?" They were gauging my level of commitment. I told them acting had been my dream since I was kid, that I'd spent countless hours lying on the floor in front of our TV watching all kinds of movies with my dad. "What acting experience do you have?" I told them all about my time at Fairmount and about the roles I'd played at Chagrin Valley.

Then they handed me a script and asked me to read. I thought I did well, but afterward, their expressions were blank and I had no idea what they might have thought. "We'll get back to you," they said, shaking my hand on my way out. Then, one of the Academy people shook my hand and as she did so, she smiled, looked me in the eyes, and nodded slightly. I took it as a clue and left feeling damn good about the whole thing.

But then came the waiting.

I was told it would be about a month before I'd hear any news, so I spent the time continuing to work at Seaway. I kept my routine going; I even kept working out. I kept running every morning, taking walks in the woods, and trying not to think about the results of my audition, telling myself that whatever happens happens, but clinging to that smile and nod I'd received on my way out of the audition.

A month came and went.

Six weeks came and went.

And then one day, I came home from work and checked the mailbox. There it was. A clean, crisp envelope addressed to me from the American Academy of Dramatic Arts. *This was it*. I felt my hands start to sweat. I tore the envelope open and began to read: *Congratulations!* That's all I needed to see. I ran for Mom and Dad to tell them the good news. I was heading back for California. This time, as an actor.

Chapter 6
Love and Death in L.A.

Dad held a farewell lunch for me at Seaway Foods where everyone wished me luck. Over the years of working for my father, I had gotten to know the other employees well, and it was great to hear everyone tell me how excited they were for me.

A few days later, I flew to Pasadena, with Dad shipping my Datsun beforehand so that it would be waiting for me. The day I left, Dad drove me to the airport. Mom held me tight at the house before Dad and I got into the car. "Promise me you'll be all right," she said, as Dad put my suitcase in the trunk. I could see tears welling in Mom's eyes.

"I promise," I said. "I'll be fine."

Dad and I talked all the way to the airport. I was excited, and he was positive and encouraging, telling me he knew I was going to be a success. I thought about all the hard times I'd given him. I hadn't been the easiest kid to raise, that was for sure. I marveled at how supportive Dad continued to be.

At the airport, we hugged at the gate, and then he turned to leave. A few steps away, he stopped and turned back around and said, "I love you, son."

"I love you too, Dad."

"Go be a star!"

I could see that he was fighting back tears. So was I. We held each other's gaze for a moment, both of us knowing that nothing more needed to be said. Then he turned and strode toward the exit, and I continued on to the jetway.

In Pasadena, I stayed at a hotel for a week before I found an apartment not far from the American Academy. It was small, but it was furnished and had everything I needed. I arrived at the school on the first day of class excited and a little anxious. I checked in and they directed me to a room with all the other students where an instructor lectured us to "work hard, be creative, and follow the rules." It suddenly felt a lot like Miami-Dade and Los Angeles Valley all over again.

Then we were separated into groups and led to different rooms where we were given tasks, starting with a page of dialogue each of us needed to memorize and perform. In all of the preparation I had done, and all the instruction I had received at Fairmount, I had neglected to prepare for a reading like this. I never practiced memorization. I was terrible at it. If I'd had more time, maybe I could have committed the dialogue to memory, but all I had were mere minutes. When my turn came, I royally fucked it up, forgetting most of what I'd been handed to read. The coach looked at me like I was an idiot, and I noticed some of the other students snickering at me. I wanted to crawl into a hole. All the students who did their reading after me seemed to pull it off flawlessly.

Next, we were given a monologue that we had to deliver while maintaining a particular posture. Even though I couldn't understand why we had to stand a certain way to deliver the lines the coach had given us, I tried as best I could. For some reason, I couldn't seem to make it work, especially after the dialogue debacle. I felt awkward, even out of place. The rest of the day dragged on, and I never felt comfortable.

I went back to the apartment that night feeling as if the day had been a disaster. Had I made a mistake in enrolling? My excitement had turned to disappointment, maybe even regret. I returned the next day and the day after that. The days became weeks, but I never felt at ease at the Academy. I stuck with it, more committed than I ever was to any other school, but as time wore on, I started getting a gnawing feeling that I really wasn't learning anything. I didn't feel as if I were growing as an actor. The place didn't give me a good vibe, I made few friends, and I could never get past the sense that I didn't seem to belong there.

For the time being, I decided to stay enrolled. What choice did I have? Was I going to quit and go back home again, like I'd done at Miami-Dade? Like I'd done at Los Angeles Valley?

I also decided to get a part-time job. I knew the year of savings I had put away wasn't going to last very long in L.A., and I found a job selling shoes at Gene Burton's Carousel, a famous, upscale clothing store for women. It was pretty easy work, and the best part was that I'd see famous actors in the store from time to time. Robert Stack would often come in with his wife. I got to talking with him one day and was surprised at how down-to-earth he was.

One day, a young woman came into the store and bought a pair of shoes from me. We talked and hit it off. Her name was Catherine and I asked her out. She said yes and one date soon turned into more. I learned that Catherine's parents were loaded. They lived in a 12,000-square-foot house in San Marino, a ritzy city just south of Pasadena. Catherine invited me for dinner one night to meet her family and there was a full waitstaff on hand—maids, butlers, a cook—it was like I was at the White House. Talk about feeling out of place.

Quickly, however, I became unimpressed. I didn't sense any love in the home. Catherine's father was older and came across as arrogant, saying very little to me the whole night, like I was somehow beneath him, like it was some great honor that they would invite me into their house for dinner. For the mother, this was her fourth marriage and it didn't take much to see that she was in it for the money. I don't think she and her husband made eye contact with each other even once the whole night.

Catherine's mother asked a lot of questions about me and about the family I came from. Apparently, she'd done her homework. She knew Dad was part owner of Seaway Foods. Whether that impressed her, with her husband's money and their 12,000-square-foot house, I had no idea. Nor did I really care. I was happy for the evening to end.

But I kept seeing Catherine. She was fun to be with, even if I didn't like her parents. We'd sometimes spend weekends at the ritziest hotels in Santa Barbara, always staying in penthouse suites. One day, driving back home through Malibu, she waved her hand out of the window and said, "You see all this land?"

"Yeah?"

"My grandfather owns it. He's a billionaire, you know." Land in Malibu? I knew her family was rich, but until then, I hadn't known how rich.

Before long, Catherine and I decided to move in together. My dinky little apartment wasn't going to cut it, though. Not for a girl like Catherine. She found us a gorgeous, four-bedroom apartment in Pasadena.

One day, Catherine's mother extended another dinner invitation to me. This time, she was having the governor over. Not only were Catherine's parents rich, they were well-connected. But I couldn't stand the thought of spending another evening in that house and I politely declined. And that's how I missed out on dining with future two-term president Ronald Reagan. First, I missed Woodstock, and now I missed dinner with Reagan. Honestly, it's hard to know what I was thinking back in those days.

Even though it was fun dating such a rich girl, it came with its share of problems. Catherine didn't have to work; she didn't have to do much of anything and didn't have a lot of interests outside of going to nice restaurants and wearing expensive clothes and spending nights in ritzy hotels. Sometimes she'd rent a Mercedes for us to drive around town in. She couldn't understand why I wanted to work or continue going to acting school. She wanted me to spend all my time with her, but her lifestyle, fun for maybe a long weekend, bored me to death. I needed to be doing something more than just hanging out. Even a day spent working in the shoe store gave me a feeling of having accomplished something, and that's what I needed. We fought a lot about it. Really, we were just two different people.

I often wondered if Catherine was happy. It didn't help that I found her family so fucked up. In this, we agreed. Catherine had a sister, too, but nobody got along with her. All her family had was money. Her parents were cold and distant. If she wanted to stop in and see them, she had to call first. It was like making an appointment. Worse, sometimes they'd tell her no. One time, we stopped by when they weren't home and Catherine grabbed us some food out of the refrigerator. When her mother came walking in, she demanded to know what Catherine was doing there without having called first, and told her she needed to pay for the stuff she took from the fridge. I was floored.

Surprisingly, her mother was always nice to me, though. Maybe too nice. I was a good-looking Italian guy, and she was in a loveless—probably sexless—marriage. I'm sure it didn't matter much to her that I was seeing her daughter. No matter what we did, I made sure never to find myself alone with Catherine's mom.

In the meantime, I kept attending the Academy, even though I never warmed up to it. The good thing was that I did get some acting gigs during that time by scouring the papers for auditions. Unlike performing at the Academy, I seemed to really shine in my auditions. There was something about a real audition that motivated and inspired me to be my best. My first role was the lead in an original, romantic play called *Beauty*. Then I landed the lead in the musical *The Fantasticks*, a popular show from that time that sold out every night.

I loved the theater. It was everything I had hoped it would be. There was nothing I had ever felt in my whole life like the feeling I got from hearing the crowd's applause. It seemed I was never more comfortable than when I was on the stage.

One evening, during my time in *The Fantasticks*, I left the apartment for that night's performance. "See you later," I said to Catherine on my way out the door.

"Goodbye, Dave," she said.

I drove to the theater, but started thinking about the tone of Catherine's voice, and the way she'd said "Goodbye." It was strange. But by the time I arrived at the theater, I'd put it out of my mind.

When I came home to the apartment that night, I smelled smoke as soon as I opened the door. I ran back to the bedroom where Catherine had apparently fallen asleep smoking a cigarette. Part of the bed was smoldering and I managed to put it out before it flamed up. But Catherine hadn't moved. Quickly, I realized she hadn't fallen asleep; she was unconscious. Then I saw the empty bottle of pills on the nightstand. Now the "goodbye" made sense. I called for an ambulance and they rushed Catherine to the hospital where they pumped her stomach. She was going to be okay.

For a week, they kept her in the hospital, moving her from intensive care to a recovery room to the psyche ward. I stayed with her the whole time. Her family didn't come at all. Not her father, not her mother, not her sister. Not even once.

I really liked Catherine, maybe even loved her. But I was young and starting a career, and I didn't need the drama. She recovered, but she continued to hold the same values—hoping I'd quit and just hang out with her all day doing rich-people things—and her family continued to be weird and distant and awful. I couldn't continue to live with her, to be a part of her life. I needed to move on. I stuck with her a few months after she got out of the hospital, until she seemed emotionally stable, and then I broke it off. She understood. I think she'd been expecting it. Then I left our gorgeous apartment and moved into a small, one-bedroom, happy for the downgrade.

Back at the Academy, I made a good friend, a great guy by the name of Michael Huddleston. One evening, Michael and I went to his cousin's Italian restaurant just outside Pasadena where we were joined for dinner by his father, David. We sat at a private table in the kitchen. I recognized David right away, and why not? At the time, David was in the midst of what would be a memorable acting career. He was a big guy, a character actor, who showed up in a bunch of TV shows like *Bonanza* and *Gunsmoke* and *Ironsides*. He found his way into movies, too. Years later, he would play "The Big Lebowski" in the movie of the same name with Jeff Bridges. Michael would go on to have a decent acting career as well, appearing in TV shows and movies.

That evening, over some wonderful Italian dishes, we talked and laughed and had a great time. David was such a nice guy, telling me how lucky he felt to have found success, and relating stories about all the famous stars he'd worked with. I went home that night feeling so stoked about Hollywood. I wanted to be a star, too. I wanted what David had.

One night, Michael took me to the Whisky. Opened in 1964, the Whisky a Go Go (its full name) is a legendary nightclub on Sunset Boulevard. All the greats have played there, including the Doors, Led Zeppelin, the Byrds, Chicago—hell, it's probably easier to list the people who haven't played there. Otis Redding recorded a live album there. So did Alice Cooper. Anyway, that night, we saw a band that was just getting its start—a band by the name of Van Halen. I was blown away. They were fucking great, and when they started pumping out albums not long after that appearance, it didn't surprise me at all that Van Halen became such a success.

My life had lately been all about acting, but that trip to the Whisky sent me back to the days of The Collection. I remembered what a trip it was to be on stage, playing rock and roll, and looking out over the screaming crowd. The people at the Whisky that night were insane in their adoration of Van Halen, and I imagined the energy those guys must have felt. I guess rock and roll had never really left me. Turned out, it never would.

Around that time, I met another girl. Linda was an actress. She was attractive and fun and full of life. She invited me to meet her parents in Beverly Hills and I found a completely different family than Catherine's. Her parents were warm and friendly. Her father, Dan Curtis, was a director and producer. He created the gothic soap opera *Dark Shadows*, and produced and directed the TV movies *The Night Stalker* and *The Night Strangler*, both starring Darren McGavin, as well as other TV movies. Eventually, he would go on to produce and direct the 1988 miniseries *War and Remembrance*, for which he would win an Emmy.

Dan was a super nice guy and he took a liking to me right away. At the time, he was directing the TV movie *Kansas City Massacre*, with Dale Robertson as FBI man Melvis Purvis, and Bo Hopkins as Pretty Boy Floyd. He invited me to watch some of the filming and I was fascinated by the process. I got to talk to some of the actors, which was a real treat. I was amazed at how they could get into their parts, how, as soon as Dan yelled "Action," they snapped into their roles, delivering their lines so believably, and with such perfect timing. These guys were pros. This is what it took to be an actor.

I continued to see Linda and we became close. She was caring and sweet and wonderful. I loved her, and I loved her family. I didn't know what was going to become of us, or where our relationship would eventually go, but whatever the future held, I never in a million years would have imagined what happened. One August, I went back home to visit my parents for a week, and I told them all about Linda and how much I hoped they'd get a chance to meet her one day soon. At one point, I called Linda's house to say hello. Dan answered the phone and he started crying as soon as he knew it was me.

"Mr. Curtis," I said, "What's wrong?"

"Linda...Linda's no longer with us," he said.

"What? No longer...what do you mean?"

"She...she killed herself last night, Dave. Linda committed suicide."

We were both crying, but through his sobs, he told me that Linda had thrown herself out of a window of the Pasadena Hilton. There was no reason, no note. Nothing. I was in the kitchen and Mom heard me crying and came in and put her arms around me, and soon she was crying, too. I told Dan how sorry I was and hung up the phone.

A couple of weeks later, after I had returned to Los Angeles, I stopped by to see Dan and his wife Norma. They invited me in, but I didn't stay long. It was strange, and sad. I asked how they were getting along. We chatted a bit, then we hugged and I said goodbye. I think we all knew that would be the last time I'd see them. It was just too painful for all of us.

Two suicide attempts, one successful. Linda's reason for committing suicide would always remain a mystery. She had everything Catherine didn't have. I would be forever struck by the randomness of the act, by the randomness of life and death. I moved on, but I would never forget Linda. A young, vibrant woman who had way too much to offer, and who left this planet way too soon.

Chapter 7

Strasberg

I wasn't getting anything out of the American Academy of Dramatic Arts, and I agonized over what to do. When I mentioned this to Michael Huddleston, he told me about another acting school: The Lee Stasberg Theater and Film Institute in Hollywood. Lee Strasberg was an actor and director, and considered to be the father of "method" acting. Method acting is where you deeply identify with your character. You understand your character's emotions and motivations. This isn't just reciting your character's lines, or even reciting them believably. This is *becoming* the character, living the character, consciously and even subconsciously.

It's no stretch to say that Strasberg reinvented the movies. He trained the likes of Dustin Hoffman, Robert DeNiro, Al Pacino, Jane Fonda, Paul Newman, Ann Bancroft, James Dean, and a bunch of other stars, including my acting hero Marlon Brando. If you watch

Brando in *On the Waterfront* or *A Streetcar Named Desire*, both from the 1950s, you'll be able to see where film changed forever. If you compare the level of acting from the 1940s with the level of acting from the 1960s, it's not even close. Once method acting entered the world of cinema, nothing was ever the same.

I learned all this almost as soon as I attended the Lee Strasberg Institute. I loved the Institute right way. Everyone was friendly and the place had a positive vibe. It felt way different than the American Academy. The Academy taught a much more technical approach. But you don't act technically; you act with your heart. Instead of doing exercises like standing a certain way while reciting lines, we were taught to take the lines and apply them to our emotions, to be totally in the moment, to *feel* what we were saying. This seemed so much more *right* to me. I learned to laugh and cry, and feel both emotions, not just act them out. We had an exercise called a "private moment," in which you did something in front of the class that you might do in private, but never in public. It's a way to be more real, to not *act*, and to therefore not look like you're acting. Method actors never look as if they're trying to act. They look authentic.

Through the Lee Strasberg Institute, I became a better actor. In class, I was getting applause, not snickers and disapproving looks from the instructor. They told me I had charisma and my confidence rose. I felt great.

I kept doing auditions, now with even more self-assuredness. I won the male leads in the theater productions of *The Unsinkable Molly Brown* and *Picnic*, enjoying every second of the performances. I couldn't quite make a living out of acting, though. L.A. was expensive and I had to keep working part-time jobs. I left Gene Burton's at one point and took a job with a flower shop in Pacific Palisades, delivering bouquets to rich people and getting paid under the table. Sometimes, I'd deliver to movie stars and other celebrities. I delivered flowers to Kurt Russell, Glen Campbell, Walter Matthau, Bobby Vinton, and more. Sometimes I had to pinch myself, unable to believe I was seeing all these famous people.

One day, I delivered flowers to Tony Franciosa, star of the movie *Career*, with Dean Martin and Shirley MacLaine. That's what I remembered him for, but he did other movies, too, and a lot of television. He'd won awards. Out on his front porch, I told him it was an honor to meet him and mentioned that I was studying acting. He confided to me that he felt his own career had stalled a bit.

I looked at his house and remarked, "It sure seems like you're doing okay."

"Yeah, maybe," he said, "but you know what? There's only one guy in this town who can *really* act."

"Oh, yeah?" I said. "Who's that?"

Franciosa pointed toward a mountain to our west, toward Malibu. "You see that house way up there?"

I made out several houses sprinkled on the distant hillside, but I assumed he was talking about the highest one. "Sure, I see it."

"The guy who lives in that house. That's an actor."

"Well...who is it?"

"Marlon Brando."

My jaw dropped.

"Anyway, nice talking to you, kid," he said. Then he went inside, closing the door behind him.

I looked back over at the house on the mountain and thought about how much respect my favorite actor got from other great actors. Franciosa won a Golden Globe for *Career*, but he didn't think of himself as being in Brando's class. In fact, he didn't think anybody was.

On another day, I met Franciosa's co-star in *Career*. I had just dropped off flowers at the Riviera Country Club, a prestigious, private club with a beautiful, Spanish-revival-style main clubhouse, built in 1928. It was gorgeous. Maybe that's why I really wasn't paying close attention to what I was doing when I backed out of the parking lot.

"Hey!" I heard a voice yell out.

I put on the brakes and suddenly, in the rearview mirror, I noticed someone behind the car. I got out and saw, to my horror, that I'd almost run over Dean Martin.

"Hey, you almost hit me there, son," Dean said in that smooth voice that anybody in the world would have recognized.

"Oh, crap, I'm sorry, Dean. I guess I just didn't see you there. I mean, I'm really sorry."

He could see I was mortified. "Yeah, well, it's okay."

I knew Dean was from Steubenville. "I love ya, Dean," I said. "I'm from Cleveland, you know."

"That's great, son. I'm just glad you didn't hit me."

"Yeah, me too. Again, my apologies."

"Sure. Take care, son."

Then Dean Martin, King of Cool, walked into the clubhouse.

I kept getting parts in stage productions and kept working part-time jobs, still hoping for my big break. A few years went by like that. And then one day I answered a casting call for a movie about the Vietnam War. Oliver Stone was going to direct it and it was going to be called

"Platoon." I was asked to read the part of "Chris," a young, naive soldier who's just been sent into action with a veteran platoon. I nailed it. Unfortunately for me, so did a young up-and-coming actor by the name of Charlie Sheen. His father Martin, of course, was a Hollywood fixture, and I knew that that didn't hurt Charlie's chances. He and I auditioned the same day and I got the opportunity to chat with him. He seemed like a really good guy. Unsurprisingly, he got the part, but if you see the movie, you'll see that he knocked it out of the park. I loved what he did with the role, and there's no denying that they chose the right actor.

Not long after that, I auditioned for a traveling theater troupe, and the audition went well. I was invited to join a group of twelve actors for four months of performances at a wonderful, old-time playhouse near Missoula, Montana. Missoula was a beautiful town, with big trees, and mountains circling the horizon. The playhouse was charming and stately. We did two dramas, two comedies, and a musical. The actors took turns playing all the different parts. One night, you might have a bit part; the next night you might play the lead. Shows were five nights a week. The theater held about two thousand people and it was packed for every show.

We'd rehearse during the two off days and prepare for the next show, but one week, we all decided we needed a break. One of the members of the troupe managed to get his hands on some psychedelic mushrooms. For a lark, I cut a hole in the middle of a blanket, threw it over my head, and played the part of a priest, giving everyone communion, placing a mushroom in each person's mouth. These were not ordinary psychedelic mushrooms. The effects lasted for the entire two days we had off from doing the play. We all sat around stoned out of our minds listening to music and feeling crazy. I bounced around between distorted feelings of euphoria and feeling as if everything was hilarious. As best I recall, I think everybody had a great time, and the effects wore off just in time for the next show.

The traveling theater experience was really special and made for a wonderful summer. The people were terrific and the time went fast. And all that experience on stage helped me back in L.A. where, shortly after returning from Montana, I auditioned for the male lead—Tony—in *West Side Story*. If I got it, it would be the biggest role I'd had yet. There must have been two hundred people there wanting parts, a dozen or more hoping for the part of Tony. When it was my turn, they had me sing "Maria." I knew I did well, but I was surprised and humbled when the director came over, held up my hand, and said, "Ladies and gentlemen, we have our Tony!"

Every night, the theater was sold out, and I was having the time of my life. One night, we did our usual curtain call to our usual standing ovation. At the end, I came out with the girl who played Maria and we did our bow to the audience. I never tired of hearing the applause. But on this night, I looked out toward the crowd and found myself overcome with emotion when I saw who was in the theater. Amid the crowd, standing and clapping and shouting my name, were my parents. Mom and Dad had flown out to see the show without telling me. They'd wanted it to be a surprise. It was more than that.

Backstage, we hugged and cried.

"Dave, you were wonderful!" Mom said.

"I can't believe you're here!" I said. "Thank you so much for coming!"

"How could we miss it?" said Dad. "You playing Tony in *West Side Story*? We had to come."

We talked some more and then, out of the corner of my eye, I noticed an older man approaching. "Excuse me," he smiled, "I hate to interrupt. Congratulations on your performance. It was outstanding."

"Thanks," I said.

"My name is Alan Presburg. I'm a producer and man-ager. Right now, I'm representing one of the best new rock and roll bands in Los Angeles. Problem is, they're in need of a new lead singer. Do you like rock and roll, Dave?"

Did I like rock and roll? If he only fucking knew.

"You've got one hell of a voice, kid," he continued. "Listen, I'll let you get back to your reunion with your folks, but do me a favor, will you?"

"Sure."

Presberg handed me a business card. "Call me tomor-row, okay? We'll talk. Congratulations again." Then he nodded to the three of us. "Good night," he smiled, before turning to go.

I glanced down at the card and my mind thought back to that night at the Whisky seeing Van Halen with Michael Huddleston and thinking that rock and roll had never left me, even with all the theater work. My in-stincts might have been right because it seemed possible that maybe—just maybe—even though I might have drifted away from it for a bit, rock and roll had found me again.

Chapter 8
ANTHEM

The studio was in north Hollywood, a small, non-descript building that sure as hell didn't look like a studio from the outside. It looked more like a small warehouse. I knocked on the metal door and a guy about my age poked his head out.

"I'm Dave," I said.

"Hey, I'm Bert. We've been expecting you. Alan says you're great. Come on in, man!"

Inside, the studio didn't look much better. It was kind of small and bare, but I was in no position to complain. Not yet, anyway. I needed to focus on the task at hand; I needed to impress these guys. Everyone introduced themselves. Bert played guitar. The other band members were David, who played bass; Clayton, who played keyboards; and Jeff, who played drums. Together, they were "ANTHEM." They were good. They played clubs around L.A. but were looking to take things up a notch and needed a lead singer. They played a couple of songs for me and I could tell right away that they had something. Then Bert handed me some lyrics to sing.

"Take your time," he said. "Let us know when you're ready."

I went off to the far corner of the room and sat in a chair and studied the lyrics. Fifteen minutes later, I walked up to the mic.

"Okay," I said. "Let's do it."

David started with a bass track, Bert jumped in with a guitar riff, then Jeff hit the drums and Clayton followed with the keyboards. Then came the vocals. I picked up on the music and the rhythm and sang the lyrics as best I could, not having ever heard the music before. My voice was strong, but I was far from perfect. A few times, I fucked it up.

We finished and I looked around the room, wondering if they were going to show me the door. But to my surprise, they were smiling. They looked at each other, nodding, then Bert said, "Okay, man, you're in. Congratulations!"

Clayton came up to me with a shoulder hug and said, "Man, you got the voice we need!"

And that was that. I was now the lead singer of an up-and-coming rock and roll band. It was strange. I had been so pumped about acting. It's all I'd wanted to do since I was a kid. But now I knew where I belonged. It felt so right. I was a born rock-and-roller. Looking back, maybe it wasn't acting I'd wanted, after all. Maybe it was *performing*. Acting was one way, singing for a band was another.

For two years we would play all around Los Angeles. Jeff eventually quit and was replaced at drums by a guy named Stovros, and we would drop David, too, who was a bit of an asshole at times, but otherwise, we stuck together. Alan worked hard and got us gigs in some great venues. But not the best ones. I thought about the Whisky. Why couldn't we play there? The Starwood in West Hollywood was another popular place that featured top-notch talent. Those were the places we needed to perform, but not just any band could get a spot. We were good, but you needed to be better than good. You needed to be great.

In fact, I started pushing for us to become better right after I joined. I wanted us to be big. I wanted us to be amazing. I'd never forgotten when I'd seen Van Halen for the first time. That needed to be us, and I didn't see any reason why, if we worked hard at it, we couldn't be on that level. I ended up taking the lead not just on vocals, but on the very direction of the band. I could tell that that's what the band needed, even more than a lead singer. ANTHEM needed to be pushed. We couldn't settle for being just another L.A. band. We needed to start thinking bigger.

It all began with the studio. I insisted on a new one. Two months after I joined the band, Alan found us a beautiful, spacious place. We had a stage put in and spotlights. Best of all, there was plenty of room for visitors to come and watch us play. Now we had a studio worthy of a great band.

I also suggested that we get a new name. I liked AN-THEM, but I felt like we could use some rebranding. I knew that branding was key. We needed a name that stood out, something unique. Something memorable. We needed a *rock and roll* name. But none of us could think of anything. "Don't worry, it'll come to us," I said. "In the meantime, we have to start rehearsing a hell of a lot more. And we need some tunes of our own. We have to write some great fucking songs!"

I set a new standard for what we should expect of ourselves, and the guys responded. Everyone got on board and started living up to the new level that we were shooting for. We rehearsed day and night and you could feel the difference. The energy was all positive and creative.

We were becoming a force.

Little by little, word got around and people started coming to the studio on weekend nights to watch us play. It's what I had hoped for when I'd insisted on a bigger studio. About 75 or a 100 would show up on a Saturday night, and we discovered they especially reacted to some of the covers we were doing. With my theater training, I did a perfect imitation of Freddie Mercury. We played "Bohemian Rhapsody" until people told us we did it better than Queen. We played "Won't Get Fooled Again," by the Who and "Roundabout," by Yes. The crowds started growing.

Unfortunately, we weren't yet making any real money. I took a part-time job once again, this time at a Hollywood men's shop selling fashionable clothing. One day, a young musician came in that I thought I recognized. He was based on the East Coast, the Jersey Shore to be exact. I followed all the new artists and I'd listened to his first couple of albums: *Greetings from Asbury Park, N.J.*, and *The Wild, the Innocent & the E Street Shuffle*. I loved his sound and so did the critics. He was adored around his hometown, but Bruce Springsteen had yet to hit the big time. Nobody could have known it then, but he was really close. I still don't know what he was doing in L.A., but I told him I appreciated his music and we got to talking. I mentioned I was from Cleveland and he said he'd played a few dates at nearby John Carroll University. Then we talked about our bands. I told him all about ANTHEM and he told me about a new album he'd been working on. "I think it's going to go," he said. "At least I hope so."

Then Bruce said he was looking for a jacket. I pointed him toward a really fucking cool leather jacket that I'd had an eye on myself. He tried it on and looked perfect in it. He paid for the jacket and we shook hands and wished each other luck with our respective musical careers.

A year later, Bruce Springsteen skyrocketed to fame with the album *Born to Run*. Half the songs on that album are still played by classic rock stations all over America. The title track alone is considered to be one of the greatest rock and roll songs in history. The best part for me? The album cover: the iconic image of Springsteen leaning against his band's saxophonist, holding his Fender Telecaster guitar, and wearing...the same leather jacket I sold him in L.A!

As for ANTHEM, we kept rehearsing and getting better. All of us. I noticed that Bert was playing guitar like Jimmy Page of Led Zeppelin. We were fucking *good*. Alan took note of our progress and encouraged it more.

He believed in us. He and his girlfriend Bonnie were always around, always positive, always our biggest fans. The management business can be risky. A lot of musical acts don't ever pan out. Alan was invested heavily in us, not only his time, but his money. He financed the studio, and he financed us, helping with personal expenses so that we didn't have to worry about anything except getting better. I would never be able to properly express to Alan my gratitude for his confidence in us and his amazing generosity.

At one point, he came up with the idea that we should all live together, and he found us a five-bedroom house just outside of L.A. I wasn't thrilled with the idea, but I went along with it. The other guys didn't seem to mind hanging out 24/7 with each other, but I needed my space. I needed some alone time. Nevertheless, for the sake of the band, knowing it wouldn't be forever, and believing in Alan as much as he believed in us, I made the sacrifice.

All the hard work over those couple of years paid off. Alan came into the studio one day and told us he'd gotten us an audition at the Starwood. We performed in front of the management and staff and we crushed it. They loved us. They gave us a date and we hit the studio hard, night and day until we felt ready—really ready.

Finally, the big night arrived—our opening night. As always, the Starwood was packed. Everyone in the band was pumped.

"Ladies and gentlemen...*ANTHEM!*"

The spotlights hit us and the crowd started to scream and applaud. We started out with our best—"Bohemian Rhapsody." I don't know if it was all the preparation or the adrenaline or what, but we'd never played it better. Everything just felt so right. When we finished, the place went nuts. We kept playing, following up with "Won't Get Fooled Again" and then "Roundabout." Soon, the crowd was chanting our name: *ANTHEM! ANTHEM!* It was an amazing night.

We had our first interview the next day and soon we were being written about in the local papers. Not long after that, I broached the subject with the guys of moving onto something even bigger. It was an idea I'd had since the day I joined the band: San Francisco. The Bay area was huge in those days. A promoter by the name of Bill Graham had put San Francisco on the map as a rock and roll destination. Along with Chet Helms, the guy behind San Francisco's famous "Summer of Love" in 1967, he'd introduced bands like the Grateful Dead and Jefferson Airplane. Chet had managed Big Brother and the Holding Company and recruited Janis Joplin as lead singer. These bands got their starts at venues like the Fillmore and the Winterland Ballroom—legendary concert halls. This was now the mid '80s, but the music was still going strong and San Francisco was musical home to the likes of Carlos Santana, Metallica, Robert Cray, Sammy Hagar, Journey, and a slew of other great artists. That's where we needed to be, and I felt that we were ready.

But there was a risk. We'd be giving up the chance to become the house band at the Starwood. This was no small thing, and it was within our grasp. Van Halen became Van Halen by being the house band at the Whisky. It had given them a chance to perfect their style and their music, all while building a huge following.

Interestingly, Van Halen had played the Starwood one night. The way I heard it, there was a guy in the audience who wanted to sign them to a record deal that very night. That guy's name was Gene Simmons of Kiss. But Gene missed his chance. He was with his manager and his manager said, "Gene, are you serious? These guys? They're never going to make it. They don't have what it takes." Gene knew better and should have listened to his gut but unfortunately for him, he listened to his manager instead.

At any rate, for us, giving up the chance to be the house band at the Starwood was worth it. San Francisco was calling, and everyone—to a man, including Alan—agreed. It was a big jump and pulling it off successfully could mean a record deal and fame. But we couldn't go as ANTHEM. I hadn't given up on the idea of rebranding, and one day, while we were playing around in the studio, it hit me like a bolt of lightning.

"Guys!" I said, "I've got it! Our new name. *Foreplay.*"

Everyone loved it. We were going to be Foreplay, and we were going to make it big in San Francisco, and then the world.

Chapter 9

Foreplay

We packed up the studio and took the Pacific Coast Highway north. While Alan was finding us a studio, we started looking for places to live. We'd grown beyond living together by then, so each of us found our own. I had some help. Clayton knew a girl in Mill Valley, just north of the Golden Gate Bridge, who had a female roommate, but could use another roommate to help defray the mortgage cost of her house. It was a great place in a beautiful neighborhood, but the best part for me were the neighbors. Carlos Santana lived next door and Grace Slick of Jefferson Airplane lived one block over. How could I say no? After I moved in, I saw Carlos out in his backyard barbecuing dinner for himself and his gorgeous wife almost every night.

Alan found a studio at Tam Junction, a big transit hub and retail center a mile and a half from my new house. We rehearsed while he went out looking for places we could play. We started writing more of our own stuff, too, something I'd thought we needed to do all along. Clayton, Bert, and I were the composers. Together, we'd write, edit, add a few lines, take out a few lines, play around with the music, lay down the rhythm, and basically keep tweaking until we got it right. I loved the creative process, and the stuff we were coming up with was solid.

Alan succeeded with his part of the bargain, setting us up with gigs all over San Francisco, and for more than a year we played in some really cool clubs. Then one day, Alan got us an opening at a place called Uncle Charlie's in Corte Madera, a hopping rock club/concert venue about fifteen minutes from Mill Valley. The owner was a woman named Jeanie. Alan convinced her to come see us play, and she liked what she saw. The next day, Alan and I went to meet with her at Uncle Charlie's and we talked and hit it off. She brought us in and soon we were performing regularly. Jeanie loved us, and we became great friends.

Others played Uncle Charlie's, too. As it happened, Huey Lewis got his start there and we were there not only to see it, but to take part in it. We played with Huey a lot at Uncle Charlie's. He was a great guy. This was before he was even signed, but everyone could tell that he had something special.

By then I had a girlfriend. To make a little extra money, I took a part-time job once again at a women's shoe store. That's where I met Pam, a customer who came in one afternoon. She was pretty and fun. I asked her out and we really clicked. Pam was a nurse who worked with elderly people, and she had a kindness about her that drew me in. We dated and before long, she moved into the house with me. She would follow me around to Uncle Charlie's and wherever else we were playing, becoming one of our biggest fans. These were great times and we were happy.

Foreplay continued playing at Uncle Charlie's, as well as other venues as the months and then years rolled by. Looking back, I don't know where the time went, but I remember some amazing moments. Alan got us a concert gig once where we opened for Steppenwolf. I got to meet John Kay, Steppenwolf's frontman and songwriter, the guy responsible for "Born to be Wild" and "Magic Carpet Ride."

Eddie Money was in San Francisco. He heard of us, and contacted Alan, telling him he wanted to work with us. Eddie was putting together a benefit concert to save a historic concert hall from being demolished. Eddie was always holding free concerts and benefit shows. For this one, thousands showed up. We played some covers but also our originals. The crowd loved us. "Foreplay! Foreplay!" they chanted. What an honor to play at Eddie Money's benefit concert. What a special night.

By then, we were recognized, and not just by people in the industry. We had fans. I noticed people in the crowd singing along to our songs. They had memorized the lyrics. Often, I'd be stopped in the street by someone who wanted to tell me how much he loved Foreplay. Sometimes they'd ask for an autograph. It was humbling. Especially so during our concerts. The chanting and the cheering were as loud as our music. I'd kneel down at the front of the stage and a sea of arms would extend toward me. After playing, we'd come down onto the floor and the crowd of people would part to let us through, touching us and high-fiving us. "We love you guys!" they'd shout. It was intoxicating, some of the best moments of my life.

Not long after the benefit concert, we played Uncle Charlie's again. Huey Lewis played that night, too. He'd been busy writing new stuff and I noticed something different about his songs. His lyrics and tunes were catchier and more melodic. His music had evolved, and I saw the enthusiastic reaction of the crowd. They loved him. I congratulated him when he came off the stage. "Man, you've put together some really great tunes!" I said.

Hours later, I lay awake in bed thinking about guys like Huey and Eddie and John Kay. They had something we didn't yet have. They had memorable songs. They had tunes people loved. I realized at that moment that it was not about how good you were or what your style was like. It was about the *song*. The song was everything. It was the song that stuck in someone's head. Where was *our* hit song?

Our stuff was good, but I knew it wasn't Huey Lewis good. It wasn't Eddie Money good. It wasn't Carlos Santana good. We needed new material. We needed new songs and new lyrics. As first ANTHEM and now Foreplay, we'd been together for five years. We had played at a lot of venues, met a lot of people, built a loyal following, and had a lot of fun. But we didn't yet have a hit.

That needed to change. I took a couple of days off from rehearsing and drove up to Bolinas, telling Pam I needed to clear my head. I'd discovered Bolinas not long before and it became the place I would always go to when I needed to get away from it all. Bolinas was a quaint coastal community with maybe a thousand people living there at the most, and they all wanted to keep it that way. The residents were known to tear down street signs that marked the way into town. And it was a beautiful drive to get there, first through the forests of Marin County and then along the water up Shoreline Highway. I felt a calming sense come over me whenever I drove to Bolinas.

Along the way, I passed Jessie Colin Young's house. With the Youngbloods, Jessie had written some great stuff, songs like "Darkness, Darkness" and "The Peace Song." On their debut album, the Youngbloods had recorded the Chet Powers song "Get Together" and turned it into a mega hit, even something of an anthem for the times. I had cassettes of the Youngbloods with me and played those songs on repeat the whole way, and thanked God I lived in this amazing musical era. I wanted Foreplay to be a bigger part of it.

When I returned, I sat down with the guys and we had a serious talk about the future. We needed to start producing hits; we needed to find a way to pull in even more fans. We needed a record deal. We couldn't keep playing in clubs like Uncle Charlie's forever. There had to be more, and everyone agreed.

A week later, we were playing at Uncle Charlie's again. Huey Lewis was playing after us, and the place was completely jammed with a long line of fans outside trying to get in. For some reason, the energy was through the roof that night, and I knew it was going to be another amazing evening. I fed off that energy and couldn't wait to play.

When I came in, I noticed a table in front of the stage with five or six guys, all with notebooks and pens. The set-up seemed a little odd, but I didn't give it much thought at the time.

The manager took the stage to announce us and the crowd went completely nuts before he could even say anything. It took him several minutes to quiet everyone enough to where he could say, "Ladies and Gentlemen, Foreplay!" Then the place *really* went nuts. We played great that night, just like always, and the fans loved every moment of it. *"Foreplay! Foreplay!"* they chanted.

Forty-five minutes after we finished, Huey came out and everybody went crazy once again. From the side of the stage, I watched as the guys at the table sat up and started paying closer attention. Now it made sense why they were there. Huey did his set—his new songs. After the first, the crowd seemed strangely subdued, and I noticed that Huey had a sort of what-the-fuck expression on his face. Then, halfway through the second song, the crowd flipped out. They hadn't been expecting new music; they hadn't known what to make of it. But once they made up their minds, the place went insane. Huey was like a god up there. And each new song was better than the one before it. Huey was playing *hits*.

Then I watched as he came off the stage, walked to the table, had a conversation with the guys sitting there, and shook their hands. As the saying goes, the rest is history.

I congratulated Huey. I smiled and told him how proud we all were of him. He'd worked hard, his songwriting had become incredible, and he deserved the break. "Way to go, man!" I said. But part of me was dying inside. Where was our break? Why couldn't Foreplay do what Huey had done? The people at that table had just seen us play at our best, and they signed the guy that came on afterward. A night that had started out so amazing quickly became heartbreaking.

I drove back to Bolinas that very night, tossing and turning in my bed. The next day, I sat on the shore and stared out at the Pacific Ocean and tried to make sense of the past several years—all the rehearsing, all the shows, all the song writing, all the hard work. Everything seemed to be leading nowhere. I didn't want to go back. I wanted to stay in Bolinas forever.

After a few days, I finally got myself together and drove back to Mill Valley.

Foreplay kept at it. What choice did we have? We just kept hoping for that big shot, that big break, our own Huey-Lewis moment. Through it all, though, we did have fun. Playing in front of the crowds was often reward enough. And every now and then, my parents would fly out to see me, and watch Foreplay in action at Uncle Charlie's. They'd take me food shopping while they were there and take the whole band out for a steak dinner, complete with beer and wine and every kind of dessert. All our girlfriends would tag along, and so would Alan and Bonnie. Everybody loved Mom and Dad.

And so, there were good times, some of the best times of my life. Being a part of a rock and roll band was amazing. But a couple of years after Huey got signed, I realized I didn't have it in me anymore. It seemed clear that we weren't going any further. We were never going to get that big shot. I sensed that we'd hit our upper limit, realizing that if the break we needed was coming our way, surely it would have already arrived.

I called Alan and told him to meet me at a restaurant in Mill Valley. He showed up with Bonnie and we sat down and I told them I'd had enough. It was the hardest thing I'd ever done, or would ever do. Eight years earlier, I had auditioned for a band called ANTHEM after Alan had spotted me in a Los Angeles theater playing the part of Tony in *West Side Story*. It had been a whirlwind since then, and I would never forget all the places we played in Los Angeles and San Francisco, and all the people we'd met, and all the good times we'd had. I hugged Alan and Bonnie and thanked them for all they had done for us. But now it was time for me to go. To where, I didn't know. I just knew the time had come to move on.

Chapter 10

Going Home

My leaving the band didn't exactly come as a shock to the other guys. Once Huey got signed, I think we all knew our days as a group were numbered. None of us were getting any younger. I was closing in on thirty. The chances of us getting signed were slim and getting slimmer. Did we want to play clubs for the rest of our lives?

The wind had come out of our sails and everyone could feel it. By the time I left, nobody had wanted to rehearse anymore. We'd stopped writing songs. We were short with each other. My break from Foreplay meant the end of the band, but that had been a foregone conclusion anyway.

I came back to the house after having met with Alan and Bonnie, and told Pam that Foreplay was no more. "There just isn't any future in it," I said to her.

"Well, what are you going to do?" she asked.

I told her I had no idea, and I really didn't. I didn't even want to think about the future. I moped around for several days, and then Pam suggested we get out of San Francisco altogether. "It might do you good," she said. "Let's go to L.A. I have an aunt with a big house in Pacific Palisades and we can live with her until we figure something out."

That sounded as good to me as anything else. San Francisco, once such a promising place for my future as a rock star, now held nothing for me but reminders of how I didn't make it. It was too painful. The dream was gone and I knew I couldn't stay.

I visited the studio once more to grab my stuff before leaving. Nobody was around. I thought about the countless practices and the crowds that had come to see us play. The studio had once been so full of life. Now it was quiet and still. I picked up my acoustic guitar and sat on the stage and began softly singing one of the songs I'd written, but I didn't get past the first two lines before I started crying. Finally, I put the guitar in its case and walked out, turning the lights off behind me and saying goodbye to a huge part of my life.

Pam and I stayed with her aunt for three months, then got an apartment in the Palisades. The area was beautiful, nestled between the Santa Monica Mountains and the Pacific Ocean, and adjacent to Malibu with the hills dotted with huge, gorgeous homes. But I was miserable. And the relationship suffered because of it. Pam and I argued over stupid shit, mostly because I was depressed and feeling sorry for myself, and I took it all out on her. But also, there was a part of her that I'm sure had wished for a boyfriend who was a rock star. Maybe that's what she'd seen in me all along. And now? Well, I wasn't that. I wasn't ever going to be that. The relationship continued to deteriorate and finally, Pam reached her limit. She walked out one day and went back to live with her aunt.

Not only was I depressed, I was now all alone. I hung around for a couple of weeks, but I knew I couldn't afford the rent on the apartment by myself. Not to mention that everything in the place reminded me of Pam. I moved to nearby Santa Monica and got a much cheaper, much smaller place—a windowless basement apartment. To this day, I don't know why I picked that one. It was dark and dreary. If you didn't open the door to look outside, you'd have no idea what time of day it was.

I guess, looking back, that's what I wanted—a dark place to mirror my mental state. I'd sit with the lights off for hours, thinking about the twelve years I'd spent in

California—first as an actor, then as a member of a rock and roll band—and how it had all come to nothing. I had no future, I had no girl, I had no life. Twenty-nine years old and it was all over.

I would doze off and sleep for hours, wake up, and go right back to sleep. I couldn't face the world. I spent days on end in my bed, covers pulled up over my head to keep the world out. One day I was awakened by a knock on the door. I had no idea what time it was, but I sure as hell wasn't in a mood to talk to anybody. I shuffled over to the door and opened it a crack to see the apartment manager standing there.

"Hey, are you okay in there?" he asked. "I've been knocking for two days."

Could that be true? I hadn't even heard him. I'd slept right through his knocks.

"Yeah, I'm fine," I managed to mumble.

"You sure?"

"Yes, I'm sure. I'm fine." Then I closed the door and went back to bed.

The next day, I went out to the front of the apartment building where there was a pay phone. I wanted to call home, but I hadn't even taken the time to order a phone for my apartment. More than wanting to call home, I wanted to *go* home. That was about the only thing I had decided about my future. There was nothing left for me in California.

Dad picked up and when I heard his voice, I started crying. "I couldn't make it," I said. "I'm really sorry, but I just couldn't make it."

"Dave," Dad said, "it's okay. Your mother and I love you very much."

But I couldn't stop crying. "My life is over," I said. My knees buckled and I fell down sobbing. I let go of the receiver and it dangled from the pay phone as I buried my head in my hands. I could faintly hear my dad's voice. "Everything's going to be okay," he was saying. "Everything's going to be okay, Dave. You'll see."

Someone knocked on the phone booth door, and I looked up to see one of the other tenants. "Hey, man, are you all right?"

"Leave me alone!" I screamed. "I've lost everything!"

The guy backed away and I kept crying.

I picked up the phone again and Dad was saying, "Look, Dave, Chuck and I will fly out there and help you pack up and we'll bring you back. What do you say?"

I pulled myself together enough to say, "It's okay, Dad. I can drive. It'll be a few days, but I'll see you soon." I cried some more then, the gravity of what I was saying suddenly hitting me. I was saying goodbye to California for good. It was all over; my dreams were dead and leaving California somehow made it official. "I'm coming home," I told Dad through my tears, then I hung up the phone and crumpled down to my knees again.

———◆———

Eight days later, I pulled up to my childhood home. It was evening. Everything looked warm and familiar, and my spirits rose a bit. Dad greeted me at the door, shouting back to Mom, "He's home!"

"Thank God!" I heard her say.

Dad and I hugged and cried, and then I hugged Mom and cried with her. We sat down and got caught up, with me telling them all about what had happened in California, the good and the bad, and the events that had led me to leave my dreams behind. We talked until 2 a.m., then I made my way, exhausted, up to my bedroom. My parents hadn't touched it since I'd left twelve years before, and it felt comfortable and safe. I felt peaceful, maybe even happy. It was good to be home and I slept better that night than I had in months.

I relaxed over the next couple of days, but it didn't take long before I started getting restless. The peaceful feeling wore off and a question reared its head, a question I'd put off ever since I'd said goodbye to Alan and Bonnie. *What the fuck was I going to do with my life?* I couldn't let it go unanswered forever. I supposed for the time being, I'd be working at Seaway Foods for Dad. But was that really going to be my future? After the acting? After the rock and roll? After the fucking *dreams?*

Depression set in, and not just normal depression. After a few days at home, I found that I couldn't seem to stop crying. And this is when I checked myself into the hospital, was transferred to the mental health facility, and was diagnosed with bipolar disorder. The treatment improved the mood swings, but wasn't of any use at all in helping me chart out a future for myself. I was still lost. I still had no idea how in the fuck I fell so hard, and how in the fuck I was ever going to get back up.

Dad kept telling me I'd figure it out. "It'll all work out, Dave," he'd say. "I believe in you." The man never stopped being my biggest cheerleader.

At Seaway, I had a sales job, wore a suit, and worked hard. I decided I was too old to be living at home, so I got an apartment. I didn't much care for what I was doing, and I didn't much care for myself. But one day, things got a little better. I went into a shoe store at the mall in Beachwood. The girl working there was named Maryann, and we talked. She was pretty and down-to-earth. An Irish girl. I somehow knew she was special, and I felt myself really wanting to get to know her. But Maryann saw me in my suit and decided I looked arrogant and cocky, and she turned me down for a date. I went back a couple of days later and asked again. Again, she turned me down. Four times I asked her out, the third was to a huge party Seaway was sponsoring with singer Robert Goulet lined up as entertainment. She still said no. I didn't quit, and thank God for that. The fourth time, Maryann gave in.

That was thirty-seven years ago and we've been together ever since.

Mom and Dad liked Maryann right away. "That's the one," they would say to me, confirming what I had already felt. They always had a great sense about these things. And Maryann loved my parents.

Before long, Maryann and I moved into an apartment in Chagrin Falls. I still had no idea what I was going to do with my life, but at least I had my girl. And it wasn't as if working at Seaway was a prison sentence. I made good money and I was becoming reasonably comfortable with the way my life was. If this was to be my complete future, well, maybe I could make it work.

Then one day I was at the office and I noticed Dad grimacing in pain.

"Dad," I said, "What's wrong?"

"I don't know," he said. "Nothing, really. Just some pain I've been getting in my back and arm. Sort of off and on."

The pain continued for days. And then weeks. Some days Dad wouldn't feel any pain at all, leading him to think that whatever it was, it couldn't be very serious. But then other days, he couldn't even stand straight up. One day, I went to visit Mom and Dad at home and saw Dad bent over in agony. We took him to the hospital where they ran a battery of tests and found nothing wrong. We went home, but over the next several months, it was clear that whatever it was, Dad wasn't getting any better. There were trips to the doctor and even more trips to the hospital. Once they even kept him overnight to run yet more tests. It was hard seeing Dad in pain, and after all he'd done for me, I would have gladly suffered in his place if I could have.

At the office late one morning, Mom called. "Dave, Dad's back in the hospital."

I knew he hadn't come in that day, and now I knew why. "What's going on?" I said.

"I'm not really sure," Mom replied. "But they've run more tests and we're supposed to meet with the doctor at two o' clock."

Mom sounded nervous. I tried not to be, but upon hearing "more tests" I felt my pulse quicken.

"Okay, Mom," I said as calmly as I could. "Two o'clock. I'll be there."

Five minutes later, the phone rang. This time it was the doctor himself telling me to be at the hospital at two. Whatever it was, it had to be serious.

I tried to think of only positive thoughts but the next couple of hours were grueling. Finally, two o'clock came around. Mom was at the hospital when I arrived and so were my sister and brothers. The doctor came out to greet us, saying very little, and then ushering us all into Dad's hospital room where Dad was lying on the bed.

"I'm sorry," the doctor said to us in the most somber voice I'd ever heard.

I looked over at Dad and could see tears welling in his eyes.

The doctor continued, "I'm afraid your father has cancer. And it's spread. There's nothing, really, that can be done."

I felt the life drain out of my body. Someone asked how long. "Weeks at the most," the doctor replied.

Everyone in the room broke down. I couldn't breathe. Dad's death sentence felt like my own. I don't remember leaving the room, but I remember that suddenly I was in the hallway, and then in my car driving insanely, driving away—away from a reality that I couldn't fathom, an impossible reality: a world without my father. My most loyal supporter. My best friend.

Chapter 11

Playwright, Shop Owner, Dreamer

It had only been a year since Dad had visited me every day in the hospital. Now, I was visiting him. The hospital became our entire family's second home. It was painful watching Dad continue to weaken—the man who had always been so strong, so outgoing, the man who had always been such a powerful presence in my life. It was just as hard watching Mom have to witness her husband's decline. I could see the sadness etched on her face and I wished like hell I could do something about it. The love my parents shared became more and more obvious with each passing day at the hospital.

Maryann and I had talked about getting married and had planned on a wedding at the Hillbrook Club, but everything came to a stop when we'd gotten the diagnosis. How could we plan such a celebratory event in the midst of my father's illness and imminent passing? But then I realized that Dad had to *be* at our wedding. How could he not be? How could the man who meant so much to me not be present when Maryann and I said our vows?

We knew that death wasn't going to wait around for us, and we knew that Dad would never make it out of that hospital room, even for the wedding of his son. So we decided we'd move the wedding up and hold it at Dad's bedside with just the family in attendance. It wouldn't be the Hillbrook Club, but what did that really matter?

One morning, the nurse came up to us and in a solemn voice, said, "I think you had better gather around your father. I don't think it will be very long now." If the wedding was going to happen in Dad's presence, we knew we needed to do it right then and there. Maryann called her parents, Mom called the priest, and in no time, we had everybody together in Dad's hospital room.

I tried to hold it together as we said our vows, but I couldn't stop the tears. The priest pronounced us husband and wife, and I watched as Dad, with all the strength he could muster, raise himself up on one elbow. Everyone's faces turned toward him. Then he opened his mouth and said, "'Bout fucking time."

The whole room broke up. It was vintage Dad. I never knew, until that moment, that a person could laugh and cry at the same time.

Dad passed a few days later. Though we all saw it coming, that made little difference. There was no way for me to prepare for his death, no way to somehow ease into it. The death came like a blow to my head. The world made no sense without my father in it and I felt as if I'd been broken into pieces.

His body was held at the funeral home for ten days where we held vigil as hundreds of people from all over the United States came to pay their respects. There was a steady line of mourners outside the funeral home that seemed to go on for blocks. Through the business, Dad had met more people than I had ever realized. But not just met. He touched these people. They came from everywhere and each one would tell me what Dad had meant to them. The stories were endless. "When I was struggling financially, your father really helped me out," someone would say. "Your dad gave me great advice," someone else would tell me. "I loved your dad," I kept hearing. I knew Dad was charming and outgoing. I knew he was a great guy. But I had no idea how respected and admired he was, or how much help he had apparently given to others. I'd always been proud of my father, but never as proud as I was those ten days. I was Chuck Lombardy's son, and that was the greatest thing I could imagine being.

After the funeral, I cried for months. It was hard to even go to the family home to see Mom because it seemed so strange and empty without Dad there. I kept expecting him to come walking through the door. Meanwhile, I had just gotten married and was trying to be a good husband. But I was filled with sadness, and Maryann had no idea what to do or say.

I kept working at Seaway, but it was difficult. I had a desk with the other salespeople in a room right across from Dad's office. The door was left open and the office remained untouched. I don't know why, maybe out of respect. I found myself going in there from time to time, sitting in Dad's swivel chair and looking at the pictures on the wall——so many pictures of us. So many pictures of Mom. I could feel Dad's presence, and yet I knew the source of the feeling was, ironically, his absence. How could he not be there? How could he be gone? None of it made any sense to me. Every time I'd go in and sit at his desk, I would end up in tears, and yet I couldn't stay away. I had to keep visiting his office, I had to find a way to feel his presence, even if it wasn't real.

One day, back in our apartment, I sat down at the kitchen table and started absent-mindedly writing Dad's name on a pad of paper. Before I knew it, a whole page had been filled. Somehow the writing helped. My mind felt a little clearer. *Writing*, I thought. Maybe that could help me channel my raw emotions. I thought back to my theater days and started writing a play. Soon, I was engrossed in it. For hours and then days on end, I wrote. In two weeks, I completed "This Time Around," a story of a young actor trying to get his first big break on Broadway. I dug into my own experiences and emotions for the story. Joey, the main character, has an explosive, rocky relationship with his girlfriend. He finds himself at odds with his chosen profession. And he's deeply affected by the recent death of his father.

I took the script to the Chagrin Theater and they agreed to let me do it. I directed and starred, and we did about twenty shows. The audiences loved it, and the whole experience helped pull me out of my grief. It was creative and healing. I gave all the profits to the Make-a-Wish Foundation. I wasn't looking to make a career as a playwright.

But what *was* I looking to make a career as? I continued working at Seaway for a year after Dad's death but being there never stopped being painful. And it didn't help that the company changed. Two more families bought into the business and the name was eventually changed to Riser Foods. I didn't care for the newcomers, and I didn't care for how big the business was getting. It wasn't the same familiar place that I'd known. It seemed to me that even more had been lost than Dad.

One day, I made one last trip into Dad's office, then I walked into the sales room and said my goodbyes to the others. "I love you guys," I said, "but I can't be here anymore. I'm out." Everyone nodded; they understood.

And then came more healing. I had lost Dad but in the midst of death came life. Maryann and I grew from two to three when our son Brandon was born, named—of course—after Marlon Brando. He seemed to me like a miracle, and I found myself moved by the idea that I was now a father. I hoped I could be as good a dad to Brandon as my dad was to me.

Needing more space, we moved out of the apartment and into a new house in Chagrin Falls. But of course, now I was out of a job. What was I going to do for a living? I certainly wasn't afraid of hard work. I'd had a job of some type ever since I was a kid. Even with the acting and with the band, I'd had jobs. But I wanted to do something meaningful, something big. I felt an entrepreneurial pull. I had a creative mind and I wanted to put it into use in my own business.

Maryann and I bounced ideas around and eventually came upon the idea of starting an upper-end women's clothing store. I had some trust money from Dad's estate, and we were sure that the idea could be lucrative. No matter what, people always wanted nice clothes. We rented some space in LaPlace, an upscale mall and opened our store, calling it Vendeé. We imported clothes from Europe and catered to the wealthy of the area. We did fairly decently in the beginning, even though it was sometimes hard to keep up with the expectations of the customer base, which wanted the best and latest finery. We made trips to Italy for merchandise, bringing back the trendiest fashions.

I liked the trips, but running the store soon turned out to be a pain in the ass. Rich women would come in, buy dresses, wear them to their country club events, put the tags back on the dresses, and then return them, telling us they changed their minds. Meanwhile, you could smell their perfume and deodorant in the material. It was infuriating. We couldn't make any money, and the rent was killing us. We moved to a smaller store in the mall, but we were still losing money. I started wondering about the future of Vendeé, and if it even had one.

In the meantime, I wrote another play, again mining from my own experiences. "Voices" was about the struggles of mental illness. I thought back to my days in the hospital—the depression, the confusion, the voices I had heard in my head. I knew firsthand the shame of mental illness. How you don't talk about it. How it becomes your secret. I wanted to write a play that could shed some light and help create some understanding. Maybe it could help people struggling with mental illness, and educate others.

When I finished the script, I wondered what an expert in bipolar disorder would think of it, and I called the Cleveland Clinic. I knew the Cleveland Clinic was more than just the best hospital in Cleveland; it was one of the best hospitals in the world. One of the staff members directed me to Dr. Herbert Meltzer. There was no one there who would be better for critiquing my play. Dr. Meltzer was not only a resident psychiatrist, but a professor of psychiatry at Case Western Reserve University in Cleveland. Today he teaches at Northwestern and is acclaimed for his research into the treatment of schizophrenia and bipolar.

I dropped the play off for Dr. Meltzer and a few days later, he called me. "I loved your play," he said. "I want to thank you for allowing me to read it. I think it's brilliant, and I'd like to know how I can help. What do you plan on doing with it?"

"I'm not sure," I said. "I suppose I could do a reading somewhere. That would probably be a good starting point."

"A reading?"

"Sure, I could get up on stage and read it, and if it's in front of an audience of the right people, maybe we could generate some interest in it."

"Well, let's do it," Dr. Meltzer said. "I'm sure I can get the right people together. Leave that part to me."

We made arrangements at the Cleveland Playhouse, and Dr. Meltzer was better than his word, inviting over 400 doctors to attend. I was stunned. Even better, about the same number of theater patrons showed up. It was much better than I had dared to hope. I read "Voices," and when I finished, the audience stood and applauded.

Afterward, I found myself surrounded by doctors asking questions and congratulating me on the work. Then a woman, one of the theater patrons, approached me and said she'd like to talk to me about funding the play. As it happened, her son, who was with her that evening, had been diagnosed with schizophrenia. She'd been lifted up by my reading and wanted to see the play come to fruition. "It deserves a stage," she said.

We set up a meeting for two days later in Dr. Meltzer's office. In the meantime, I learned more about the woman. It so happened that she was worth millions. Just what we needed.

The woman brought her attorney, and I brought my older brother who came with an attorney he had used before. Dr. Meltzer had an attorney present from the Clinic. There was a lot of legal firepower in the room but unfortunately nothing came of it. As it turned out, the woman wanted to buy 100 percent of the play. She wanted it all. She'd keep my name as author, but that was it. I wanted to see the play get staged. I didn't care about the money or about ownership interest, but I wanted at least a *piece* of it. Something. It was my play, after all, and it was near and dear to my heart. I asked for 10 percent. She refused. It was all or nothing. And with that, the meeting came to an end.

I thanked Dr. Meltzer for all he had done and we promised to keep in touch. I knew that if that woman had had that much interest in the play, maybe someone else would too. I wasn't going to give up on "Voices."

For the time being, however, I had other obligations. Maryann and I were still running Vendeé, we were still losing money, and I was still losing patience with the customers. But not all of them. Maryann and I got to know a man by the name of Paul Seegott and his wife Betsy, who would often come into the store. Paul owned a lot of real estate around Chagrin Falls and took a liking to us. He seemed to appreciate my entrepreneurial spirit, even if the business wasn't exactly making us rich. In fact, I confided in him one day that the store had been a struggle.

"You want to keep running it?" he said.

"I don't know," I said. "I guess, to be perfectly honest, I really don't. But what else can I do? I don't want to work for anyone else."

"What's your background?"

"Well, my father was in the food business. He was part owner of Seaway Foods."

"So how come you're not in food?"

"I was at one time. I worked for my dad for quite a while, even as a kid. But not long ago, he passed away. I left the company and my wife and I figured we could make this clothing thing work."

Paul was thoughtful for a moment and then said, "Tell you what. I've got a small property in downtown Chagrin Falls. Right on River Street. Retail space. Cheaper than here. It's not very big, but it would definitely suffice for a small retail store and right how it's sitting empty. Why don't you figure out what you want to do, and come see it?"

Paul's retail space, sitting on the Chagrin River, was next to a Starbucks and came with a quaint, red, 320-square-foot house that at one time had been a gas station on the other side of town. Paul had liked the little house and had moved it to the property. Maryann and I decided that we liked the location and rented the space, using the little red house as storage.

Unfortunately, things got no better for us. And even if they would have gotten better, I had, by then, lost all interest. I didn't want to sell women's clothes. I had no passion for it.

I felt stuck.

Then one day, in 1997, I walked out back of the store and stood on the deck, looking over a parking lot at the little red house. And that's when it hit me. Like a lightning bolt. I thought about Paul saying, "How come you're not in food?" I thought about something else, too. I thought about those amazing sandwiches Dad and I used to make ourselves at night in the kitchen of our home when I'd come home late. The idea came together in a millisecond.

"Maryann!" I said, calling from the deck. "Come out here!" I pointed to the little red house and said, "What do you think?"

"What do I think about what?" Maryann said.

"Look at it."

"Look at *what?*"

"The house! Don't you think that would make a great sandwich shop?"

Maryann looked at me like I was insane. "Huh?"

"Oh, yeah, I can see it now," I continued, my excitement growing. "But not just any sandwich shop. No, no, a really *cool* sandwich shop. A *rock and roll sub shop!*"

"You know what I think?" Maryann said. "I think you're out of your fucking mind." Then she gave me a kick and went back inside.

And that's how it all began.

Chapter 12

My Angels

The rock and roll theme was a must. It couldn't be just a sub shop. It had to be a rock and roll sub shop. Rock and roll had been a huge part of my life, and it still was. I wasn't playing it anymore, but it hadn't left me. It helped define me, in fact. It was part of who I was and where I'd come from and the times I'd grown up in. And now, with the shop, I had the opportunity to express that, to express my real self. My business could not be separate from my lifelong state of mind.

But there was another element that I knew was necessary: the quality of the product. Those sandwiches Dad and I shared over the kitchen sink when I was a teenager were built with the best stuff around. I had to replicate that. I wanted to create sandwiches that customers would remember, that customers would come back for time and again. Nothing less would suffice.

First things first. I needed to decorate the place, immerse it totally in a rock and roll vibe. I wanted it to ooze rock and roll. I mentioned my plans to Paul Seegott. Seeing as he was my landlord, I figured he'd want to know. Paul listened and said, "Dave, whatever you want to do. Just let me know how I can help." By then, Paul had become much more than a landlord. He'd become a good friend, and he wasn't kidding about helping. Paul owned a $130 million chemical distribution company. His local real estate holdings represented only a part of his wealth. Paul believed in me and my idea, and loaned me the money for the build-out, the equipment, and even the food to get us started. The idea was that we would be partners. Paul was amazing. Eventually, he would give me the whole business, saying that I could pay him back whenever I could. "Dave's is all yours," he told me. We would ultimately pay Paul back, but he never asked for it and he didn't even make us sign a note. It was all on a handshake.

The house had a peaked roof. There was no second floor, so that meant the ceiling of the shop was peaked, too. I hired an artist, a woman with wonderful talent, who came in and painted the ceiling turquoise, then painted the faces of rock and roll legends who had passed away: Jimi Hendrix, Elvis Presley, Jim Morrison,

Janis Joplin, Buddy Holly, Keith Moon, John Lennon, and several others. Then she painted the rest of the shop in bright, vivid colors. Things were taking shape.

After the painting, I put up posters everywhere of rock stars, concert billboards, and newspaper clippings. I had pictures of the Beatles, the Rolling Stones, Led Zeppelin, and, yes, even a few pictures of Foreplay rocking out at Uncle Charlie's. I hung several guitars on the walls. I even hung a drum set. Needless to say, I had classic rock playing through the speakers. The interior of the house was completely transformed. It was electric. The Rock and Roll Hall of Fame, just twenty-four miles up the road, had nothing on my shop.

Now it was time to begin the quest for a quality sandwich, and not just quality—I wanted to make the best sub in the state of Ohio, maybe in the country. I drove around and hit twenty-five of the most popular sub shops of the greater Cleveland area, collecting Italian subs and other types of sandwiches from each and every one. Then I sat down at my kitchen table and took them apart, examining every ingredient. All the sandwiches were good, but none of them was great. None of them rivaled the subs Dad and I used to make. My years at Seaway had educated me about quality food. The key in my mind was the bread, and none of these shops used great bread. Moreover, the meats were mediocre. The sauces were plain. The peppers and tomatoes were ordinary. That's when I knew I could not only compete in the sub business, I could rule.

I got all the best breads and meats and cheeses I could find, most of it from Sysco Corporation, a distributor of fine foods that I knew well from my time at Seaway. The bread they presented me with was perfect——flavorful and crunchy and soft——and it became my bread. Literally. It was now exclusive to my sub shop. Nowhere else in the Cleveland area could you find the bread that I was going to use for my subs.

I also went around to local grocery stores looking for the best peppers and onions and tomatoes and other fixings. Then I went to work on what would eventually become our signature sauce: the perfect combination of red wine vinegar, garlic, onion, pepper, and spices. I played around with the recipe until I finally arrived at something positively orgasmic.

I worked on the menu and created a list of sandwiches, giving them names like "The Original Dave's Italian," "The Turkey Dave," "Dave's Peace Steak," "The Grateful Dave," "The Far Out," "Dave's Haight-Ashbury," "The Crazy," "The Meatball," and "Dave's Tuna." Here's the thing about these subs: for the most part, they were identical to the subs my father and I made—sandwich inventions from almost thirty year prior, waiting patiently all that time to be introduced to a hungry public. I only wished Dad could have seen what I was now doing with our subs.

I wrote the names of the subs on a big board that I hung above the counter. Then I hired a woman named Sandy to make the subs, training her on *exactly* how to put them together. They had to be just right, especially when it came to the quantities of the fixings and signature sauce, which would eventually be called "Dave's Cosmic Sauce."

Apparently, though she'd never admit it, Maryann didn't think the idea of the shop was so fucking crazy anymore. Seeing my passion, she came aboard immediately. Maryann saw what I was doing and just *got* it. She understood right away that what I wanted to do was create not just a great sub, but a human connection with the customer. A memory, an atmosphere, a vibe. Together, we worked hard to make the dream happen.

Finally, we were ready to open, and it couldn't have come too soon. Money was tight and getting tighter. At one point, we couldn't pay the electric bill for our house and the electric company cut off the power. Once again, Paul came to the rescue. I don't know how we would have made it without him. And not just financially. Paul was a man of faith, and his faith rubbed off on me. I began to believe that all things were possible. Paul Seegott was an angel.

To little fanfare, "Dave's Famous Subs" opened on March 5, 1997 in Chagrin Falls, Ohio, in that little red house. We picked up customers who happened to be passing by. But the first couple of weeks, I noticed how each one reacted when they came into the place. Their mouths hung open as they gazed around at the walls and ceiling, their attention captured by all the little details of the décor that we had been so careful to choose and display. Often, they'd talk about rock and roll, the pictures and paraphernalia reminding them of great music and great memories. They'd tell me about some special concert experience they'd had, or some album from years ago that they'd played until they had worn it out. People would tell me about the first record they ever bought, or maybe the first stereo they owned.

Then they would order, and the experience would get only better. After a while, I stopped counting the times a customer would say, "Dave, that's the best sub I've ever had!"

I had room for only two tables inside, but I had benches outside. Some customers would stick around to eat their subs, some would take them outside, and some would order them for takeout. But the one thing they all had in common was that they quickly became repeat customers. Within the very first week, I started to see the same people. It was extraordinarily gratifying, confirmation that my idea was a winner. Soon, word of mouth got around, the best advertising in the world. Within a couple of months, Dave's Famous Subs was rarely without a line of customers queued up to order lunch or dinner. I had no choice but to hire more sandwich makers.

Nevertheless, I had friends (and even family) who told me that our shop would never be really successful. My rich friends would all say something along the lines of, "Yeah, I suppose you can probably make some kind of a living from it." I hated the condescension. These were people who felt they were above running anything as common and ordinary as a sandwich shop. But I knew we could do a lot better than "make some kind of a living." I knew our shop could be great, and I knew we could prove them all wrong.

And so, Maryann and I kept at it. Although we were equal partners, we knew our respective strengths. I was the face out front, mingling with the customers, and she ran the back, keeping everything moving and organized.

Together, we worked at the shop from 10 a.m. to 10 p.m., seven days a week.

In addition to making the subs, Maryann made sure our standards were always met, that cleanliness was always maintained, and that nothing but quality ingredients were used in our sandwiches. She hired and managed the employees, too. Dave's would never have been Dave's without her.

Things got a little harder when our beautiful daughter Rachael was born, but we managed to make it work. Somehow, even with two children now, we were able to put the time into Dave's that it needed to succeed. Where we got the energy, I'll never know. I suppose the customers kept us energized. And the kids did okay. Brandon even worked at the shop for a while when he got older. Today, Brandon and Rachael are two grown, successful adults that we couldn't be prouder of.

One day, an older gentleman walked into the shop. Like most people, he paused and looked around at all the paraphernalia. But he took his time. I only needed a second to recognize him. Everyone in Cleveland, and certainly everyone in the rock and roll world, knew who Myron "Mike" Belkin was. With his brother, Jules, Mike was a legendary concert promoter. Mike was also a successful manager, and he'd managed the likes of the

James Gang and Wild Cherry. He also managed the Michael Stanley Band. In fact, it was Mike who put Michael out front. Mike was around from the beginning of the rock and roll industry, and it was his promotion of rock concerts in Cleveland that helped secure the city's reputation as such a rock and roll destination, the self-proclaimed capital of rock and roll. Mike wasn't afraid to take risks. He brought in everybody. If there was a famous band, or a band that was on the cusp of fame, Mike arranged for them to play Cleveland. It's no exaggeration to say that without Mike Belkin, Cleveland wouldn't have been on anyone's radar as the place to house the Rock and Roll Hall of Fame. With Mike's work and forward thinking, Cleveland became the no-brainer location for the museum.

Interestingly enough, when the Belkin Brothers started out in the late '60s, they rented office space from a building Uncle Lester had built. I remember going to that building as a kid and seeing the Belkins. It was a modest little business they were running at the time, and of course I had no idea who they would become and how important to the city of Cleveland they would be. And there's no way in hell I could ever have imagined that one day, Mike Belkin would be standing in a rock and roll sub shop that I owned.

Mike gazed around the shop, looking up at the ceiling and around at the stuff on the walls, taking it all in. Then he stepped to the counter.

"Are you the owner?" he asked.

I nodded.

"Well, I love your shop." He put his hand out. "I'm Mike Belkin."

"I know," I said, shaking his hand. "Everyone in Cleveland knows who you are. This is a real honor. Oh, I'm Dave. Want a sub?"

"No, thanks, I just had lunch. I was just walking by and wanted to see what all the fuss was about. My office is just a block away. You guys sure stay busy."

And that's how my relationship with Mike Belkin started, my second angel. Mike came around often. Sometimes, when he'd have important meetings in his office, he'd call and order ten or fifteen subs or more at a time. Always, he had great ideas for the shop that he would share with me. It seemed that most of the times we'd talk outside. I'd be leaving the shop for some reason or another, and he'd be coming by and we'd both stop and chat, usually in the parking lot of the nearby CVS. It seemed that every time we talked, I'd learn something from Mike.

One day, we were chatting and I told him I'd gotten wind of a new chain of barbecue restaurants named Famous Dave's.

"Maybe I should change the name of the shop," I said. "I was thinking of something with the word 'cosmic.'"

"Of course," Mike said. "Because you're Cosmic Dave."

"I'm what?"

"Cosmic Dave. That's who you are." Mike said it like he'd known it all along. I wasn't just Dave, he explained. I was *Cosmic* Dave. "And the subs," he continued, "are Dave's cosmic subs."

I was blown away. It was the perfect name. That day, Dave's Famous Subs became Dave's Cosmic Subs.

"You should trademark the name," Mike suggested. "And not just for the state. You need a federal trademark. For the entire United States. You could go national someday." Mike was thinking big. That's what he did. He knew we had a great theme and a great menu, and he didn't see any reason to limit it to Ohio.

And then he came up with another idea. "Give the subs away," he said.

"Do what?"

"For, like, two hours. Pick a day and advertise that for two hours all subs are free. What will it cost you? A few hundred bucks? A few thousand? Think of the new customers you'll gain. One free sub to someone who's unfamiliar with your shop could mean a loyal customer who eventually buys dozens or even hundreds of subs."

I loved the idea. I took Mike's advice and picked a two-hour window the following week and we got the word out. The reaction blew me away. People lined up for blocks. It happened to rain that day, but it didn't matter. People stood there with umbrellas. It could have snowed and I think they would have still lined up. We gave two thousand subs away, and Mike had been right; it was the best publicity imaginable. We made a shitload of new customers, many of them becoming lifelong patrons of, and advocates for, Dave's Cosmic Subs.

Unfortunately, we weren't making many friends with the local business owners. Chagrin Falls was a conservative town. My shop's hippy, rock and roll theme was a little too far out for the other downtown establishments. I hadn't realized the extent of the resentment until we painted the exterior front of the shop. Eric was an employee but also something of an artist and I gave him free reign to do what he wanted. Eric took an afternoon and painted the façade in vivid, psychedelic colors, with a big peace sign painted right over the door. It was beautiful, and I was thrilled.

Apparently, however, someone was watching Eric paint because not more than a half-hour after he finished, I got served with papers from the town council. I was going to have to appear in court. The painting supposedly violated some ordinance and unless I complied, they were going to shut my store down. I was floored. I figured there had to have been some mistake. I went outside and stood in the street looking at Eric's work. It was perfect; it reflected exactly the theme of the shop. And they were going to shut me down? I walked around the back of the store and sat on a rock by the river and cried. I had worked so hard on the business—to make it what it was, to convey the theme not just of the shop but of my life. Dave's Cosmic Subs represented me. They weren't threatening to shut the shop down; they were threatening to shut down *me*.

I felt demoralized and I prayed to God for help. I finally pulled myself together and went inside and called the mayor. Thomas Brick had been into the shop. I'd given him free subs, and he and his wife were fans. Maybe Mayor Brick could help, I figured. He had to. Somebody had to.

The mayor was out, but the girl answering the phone in his office promised he'd call. In less than five minutes, the phone rang.

"Dave, what can I do for you?" Mayor Brick asked.

I was still emotional. "They want to shut me down," I explained. "My business!" Then I told him about the new paint job on the front façade and the notice I'd been served with. "How can they do that?" I asked.

"Dave, sit tight," he said. "I'll be there in five minutes."

Mayor Brick lived in a big house a few blocks away. He came over in even less than five minutes and stood outside the shop looking at Eric's work. I watched him from the register as he gazed thoughtfully at the façade for several minutes. Then he waved me outside to join him. I was sure he was going to tell me I had to abide by the town council's order. It was unfortunate, he'd say, but a town ordinance is a town ordinance.

Instead, Mayor Brick turned to me and said, "The peace sign."

"The peace sign?" I said. "What about it?"

"Paint over one of the bars so it's not a peace sign anymore. That'll make the whole thing less...hippy-ish."

"That's it? That's all I need to do?"

"Sure, that'll do it." Then he took the papers I'd been served and tore them up.

And that's how Mayor Thomas Brick became my third angel. Somehow, the local paper picked up the story and ran a headline that said, "Mayor Brick Saves Dave's." The publicity brought even more people into the shop. I knew that the town council members had to have been beside themselves.

Not long after that, Dave's Cosmic Subs was featured in *Cleveland Magazine*. Eventually, we'd be voted the number one sub shop by the readers of that same magazine. We'd be voted number one in *Scene* magazine, too.

And we weren't done. Dave's Cosmic Subs was only starting out. But none of it would have happened without my three angels: Paul Seegott, Mike Belkin, and Thomas Brick. To this day, I don't know what I did to deserve such valuable help. All three were successful businessmen, and, honestly, I think they saw a little of themselves in me. Like me, they had all started out at one time with probably nothing more than their dreams. Maybe they'd each been given breaks, too. Maybe helping me was their way of paying things forward, to give someone like me a leg up. Three wonderful men. Three great friends.

Chapter 13
My Crazy Idea Grows

Mayor Brick's rescue and the ensuing publicity helped propel Dave's into the stratosphere. We would open every morning at 10:00 a.m. and there would already be people lined up outside the door just waiting to soak in the ambience of Dave's and taste something great from our menu. We had four sub makers and they stayed busy all day long. There was never a letup. Besides the people in line, the phone rang constantly with orders. Some were companies or organizations or schools, ordering dozens of subs at a time. Lunchtime was packed. I took orders and greeted people coming into the shop while a symphony played in the background of lively banter, laughter, and rock and roll.

Everybody knew my name. "Hey Dave!" they'd shout out. "It's Cosmic Dave!" "You're the man, Dave!" "Love your subs!" Magazines and newspapers were starting to write about us. They'd want to interview me and I'd have to answer their questions at the same time I was running the register, calling out orders, and joking with the customers. If I took a break and went somewhere for fifteen minutes or a half hour or so, which wasn't very often, I'd invariably receive a round of applause when I returned. It was humbling and gratifying. Dave's Cosmic Subs was a big success. And along with the success came the money. Maryann and I had come a long way since the days when we couldn't pay the electric bill.

Above all else, we worked hard to make certain the shop was living up to our principle core value: to spread peace and love through our subs. In fact, that became our mission statement, and we made sure every employee understood it: "To spread love around the world one sub at a time—love of great food, love of people, and love of rock and roll." That mission manifested itself in the energy of the place. People's moods changed when they walked through the door. Ours was an oasis of positive, feel-good waves. It was what Maryann and I set out to do from the day we opened. And we did it together as one.

More than anything, I loved the creative part of the enterprise. I've learned there's creativity in everything, whether it's playing music, writing plays, or inventing sandwiches. Sometimes I'd be working the register when I'd be struck by an idea for a new sub. "Maryann!" I'd call out, "I got a new sub!" She'd run to the board as I'd describe the ingredients before the idea slipped away: "Dave's sauce, mayo, turkey, cheddar cheese, hot peppers, lettuce, blue cheese! We'll call it 'The Blue.'"

Another time: "Prosciutto, capicola, hot pepper, lettuce, tomatoes, onions, provolone, herbs, Dave's Sauce! We'll call it '"The Crazy'!"

This happened regularly.

Things continued to roll along and then one day, two years after our shop's debut, a gentleman approached me at the counter. "I'd like to talk to you," he said, in a low voice, motioning me to the side.

"Sure," I said, taking a few steps closer to him. "What about?"

"I love your shop."

"Thanks."

"I love the concept."

"I appreciate that. We try."

"And I'd like to open more of them."

"You'd like to open more Dave's Cosmic Subs shops? Like this one?"

"Yes. In fact, I'd like the rights to open 250 of them."

My jaw dropped. Two-hundred and fifty shops? Was this guy for fucking real?

"If you're interested, bring your attorney to my place and we'll discuss the details."

He left me his address and a time to meet. I checked the address out. A 10,000 square-foot house in the exclusive Shaker Heights neighborhood. It was like a palace. Yes, apparently the guy was for real.

I went there with my older brother and listened to what the man had to say. He repeated how much he loved the concept of Dave's. It was unique and had national potential. I thought about what Mike Belkin had said about expanding. Here was our chance. The man told us he was willing to put up all the money in return for fifty percent of the income. Then we parted, with him promising to be in touch with a written proposal, and me promising to think it all over. We planned to meet again in a couple of weeks.

It never happened. Several days later, I read in the paper that the man was arrested for embezzling. Ultimately, he went to jail. What were the odds that the one guy interested in investing so much in our concept would be arrested? So much for the 250 stores.

Naturally, I was disappointed. Then again, I was also relieved that I hadn't gotten into bed with a crook. The good thing that came out of it was confirmation of the idea of growing big. What was stopping us from scaling up? And that's when the idea of franchising hit me. The Dave's Cosmic Subs theme could work anywhere.

We got the word out that we were looking for franchisees and before long, a couple of guys came along who were interested in opening our first franchise shop. They were good guys, sincere, and eager to get started. We agreed on a price, and an ongoing percentage that I would take of the profits. But there were rules. First, the shop had to be decorated just like ours. We had developed a brand and it needed to be followed. Without branding, you have nothing. I'd learned that working at Seaway.

Just as importantly, the quality of the product had to be up to our standards. That meant the ingredients had to be the exact same. I wasn't willing to take a chance that inferior meats or cheeses would be used, and, in fact, I decided that part of the deal was that they had to buy the food directly from me. That way, I could ensure that someone buying a sub in the franchise store could expect the same exact quality experience as what they would get at the original Dave's.

The new shop opened at Fairmont Circle near John Carroll University, and it did well right from the start.

Soon, we opened more shops. In no time, Dave's Cosmic Subs became a household name all over the Cleveland area, and before long word spread all over Ohio and beyond. It was exciting watching the concept take off.

We continued to receive great publicity too——articles and reviews in all the major papers and local magazines. People from out of town would make a point of stopping by to order a sub, especially from our shop——the original 320-square-foot "Dave's." They'd heard of us before they'd even come into town. Some of the people were famous, people that could have eaten anywhere. But they'd either read or been told about our subs, and they wanted to know if the menu lived up to the hype.

A *Rolling Stone* reporter came in one day. In the next issue, they reported that Dave's Cosmic Subs had the best tuna sub in the country. In the country!

David Letterman was in town one night to catch a play that his girlfriend's mother was in. He came into the shop and asked me what was good. I couldn't believe he was standing right in front of me.

"What do you like?" I asked.

"Well, I love a good meatball sub."

"Then you'll love ours."

Letterman took the sub outside, came back in fifteen minutes, and said, "Best fucking meatball sub I've ever had."

I smiled and held out my hand. "I could use a few hundred grand to go national. We're expanding, but a little seed money wouldn't hurt."

Letterman laughed. "Listen, I got enough problems right now with the network. But keep up the good work. Your place is great."

One day, Geraldo Rivera came into the shop. He'd recently moved into a big house in Shaker Heights, previously owned by the CEO of Sherwin Williams. Geraldo wasn't originally from Cleveland, but he'd adopted it as his home. Like Letterman, he looked at the menu board and asked what was good. I gave him some suggestions but he couldn't make up his mind.

No one else was in the shop at the time, but soon, while Geraldo was trying to decide what to order, people started trickling in. Everyone recognized him. Everyone except the new girl I had working with me behind the register. "That's Geraldo Rivera," I said to her under my breath. "Who?" she said. Geraldo overheard and frowned a little, but then his attention went back to the board.

The next thing I knew, there was a crowd trying to squeeze into the shop. Meanwhile, Geraldo kept hemming and hawing about what he'd like to eat.

Finally, he said, "How's the tuna sub?"

"It's great," I said, and I mentioned *Rolling Stone*'s opinion. "Best in the country."

"Then make it a tuna."

I took his order, he stepped aside, and I asked the next person in line.

"Yeah, I'll take the tuna, too."

"Me too," said the next customer.

"Tuna for me," said the one after that.

Everybody ordered a tuna sub that day.

I handed Geraldo his sub and said, "See what you did?"

All the while, we kept opening new franchise locations. I would explain to the new franchisees what we expected of them and make sure they were on board with the whole concept, then I'd turn them over to Maryann who would handle all the paperwork and make sure they'd get set up properly. We'd help them in any way we could.

Ultimately, Dave's would have twenty-eight locations in four states, including Vermont, New Hampshire, Georgia, and California. We became a multimillion-dollar organization, something I could never have even dreamed of when we started.

But of course, it was a lot of work. We had to babysit the franchisees and make sure they were adhering to our standards. One time a location in Macedonia, Ohio ran into some management problems. By then, I'd had a loyal employee named Geri Linz who had started out as a part-time cashier and had moved to sub maker and eventually manager. She came to me and said that she and her husband Mike would be interested in buying the Macedonia location and turning it around. I knew if anyone could do it, it would be Geri. Maryann and I really wanted to see her succeed. The four of us spent weeks remodeling, hanging new pictures all over the walls, and revamping the kitchen.

Geri's location opened and business boomed for her. I'd visit from time to time, and every time I did, I could see how clean the store was and how smoothly she and Mike were running it. And I noticed the line out the door, too, just like at our original shop. I wished all my franchisees were as effective. It was wonderful to see someone who had originally come to work for me on a part-time basis——basically, as she put it, "to get out of the house"——succeed in such a huge way with a store of her own.

Meanwhile, I continued to get closer to Mike Belkin. With his mentoring and encouragement, he was becoming like a second father to me. I also got to know his son, Michael, who had joined his father's business years before. Michael was every bit as wonderful and supportive as his dad. One day, he came into the shop and made an observation that stuck with me. There were a lot of photos and posters on the walls of the shop that represented Northern California bands—Jefferson Airplane and Quicksilver Messenger Service and other psychedelic rock bands from the San Francisco Bay area. "Dave," he said, "why don't you localize this more? People in Cleveland want to see some Cleveland artists. And then you can use that same 'local' concept around the country, wherever you open a new place."

I thought it was a great idea. I also thought it might be nice to find a way to show my appreciation for all Michael and his father had done for me. I had been to their offices and I'd seen all the photos on their walls of the Belkins with every great rock and roll star imaginable. Pictures of them with the Rolling Stones, Elton John, you name it. I asked him if I could put some of those on the walls of the shop. One Saturday morning, I met Michael in his office when no one else was around, and went through his collection of photos and posters.

I told Michael not to tell his dad what I was doing. Back at the shop, I stripped one whole wall of everything that was on it, and replaced it all with Belkin photos, floor to ceiling. It was impressive. I had a sign up top that said "Dave's presents Belkin Productions." We called it "The Belkin Wall."

A few days after that, Mike came in with Michael. As usual, the shop was crowded. We chatted a bit like normal, even though it was everything I could do to not blurt out what we had done. I wanted Mike to notice it on his own. He ordered his sub, then turned to pay, and that's when he saw it. He froze, gazing at the wall for several seconds, not saying a thing. Then he took a step toward it and he looked around at all the pictures. He noticed the sign up top and grinned. Finally, he turned to me and said, "I love you, man."

"Ladies and gentlemen," I said to everyone in the shop, "The Belkins!" The place erupted in applause.

I had one more surprise for Mike. I pointed to the menu board at a new sub we'd created: The Belkin. Pastrami, salami, and Swiss cheese. It was Michael's favorite. In fact, it was all he ate for years. By then, his dad was on a veggie diet, but he still appreciated the thought. The Belkins were now officially immortalized in Dave's Cosmic Subs. The funny thing is, Michael would sometimes ask how the namesake was selling. I had to be honest; people around Chagrin Falls were too damn health conscious. "It's my worst seller!" I'd tell him. But I wasn't about to stop offering it.

All the while, the publicity surrounding Dave's continued to grow. The *Chagrin Solon Sun* did a piece on us. So did the *Akron Buzz,* a periodical that was always interviewing famous celebrities. I was flattered that they wanted to interview me. I was also interviewed by the *Cleveland Plain Dealer*, too. The reporter, Sarah Crump, asked how we made our special "Cosmic Sauce." I told her that you take some of Jimi Hendrix's purple haze, jump on the magic carpet ride, and when you're done with your magical mystery tour, you'll know. That description went into the article. *Thrillist* wrote a piece entitled, "How Dave's Cosmic Subs Became the Sandwich Mayor of Cleveland." People recognized me on the street and it was gratifying to know that our shop meant so much to them.

At one point, a competitor's shop opened near our franchise shop in the Atlanta area. The shops were just off the Emory University campus, and the students preferred ours hands down. *The Emory Wheel* did a piece on Dave's, defining the two shops succinctly: "One is corporate, the other is charm." Customers were interviewed and they all said the same thing: Dave's was "100 percent hands-down" better than the chain shop. They would come for the sandwiches and stay for the vibe. Dave's became a popular hangout and nothing could rival its energy, which was extraordinarily gratifying to hear because it was exactly what we were going for. I also thought about those college kids and their interest in a restaurant based on a rock and roll theme. Maybe there was hope for the younger generation. Neil Young was right: Rock and roll will never die.

The Dave's in California got similar publicity in the *Sun*, and it's become a favorite place to hang out along the Pacific Coast Highway just south of Long Beach.

Sure, maybe Dave's started out as a crazy idea, but don't all great ideas? Everyone thought the Wright brothers were crazy, too. Sometimes, with enough passion, you can get your ideas to work. Crazy can be a launching pad for success. And, really, when you stop and think about it, yes, the idea was a little out there, but the formula couldn't be any more straightforward: *peace, love, and subs.* How could I miss?

Chapter 14

How I Did It

Dave's Cosmic Subs has been in operation for almost three decades. Today, people frequently ask what the secret was to our success. Often times, a young entrepreneur will seek me out to pick my brain. How did you manage to do it? they'll ask. Although I'll never divulge the ingredients in Dave's Cosmic Sauce, I'm happy to divulge the ingredients that made up my success. It's a simple recipe, really, and anybody can duplicate it: passion and hard work.

I don't think you can do anything successfully unless you have a strong passion for it. If you're doing something just to make money, with no real love for it, you're never going to succeed, no matter how hard you work. And even if you enjoy some initial success, you can never keep it going without truly loving it. Maryann and I made *a lot* of money with Dave's. But money was never my first interest. What drove me was the idea of making the absolute best subs in an atmosphere of love and peace and rock and roll. We provided more than food. We provided a vibe, and it was a vibe that represented the best of me, the best that I could offer the world. It was who I am. It was real and genuine, and it resonated with every person who came through the door. It's what drove me.

That vibe, by the way, could not have been anything else but what it was—sourced in one thing and one thing only: rock and roll. The time I spent in California—writing music, playing concerts, hanging with the likes of Huey Lewis and Eddie Money and John Kay—stayed with me. The concerts, especially. The crowds and the cheering and the energy. Playing at the Starwood. Playing at Uncle Charlie's. Even playing in our studio to the hundred or so fans that would pack the place. All of that moved me. It became a part of me. That's why, when I looked over at the little red house from our clothing store that fateful day, the vision that popped into my head was not just the vision of a sandwich shop, but a *rock and roll* sandwich shop. It could not have been anything else.

I was so passionate about what I had created that I would never have stopped doing it, even if it had failed. I would have tried again. And again. If you're passionate about something, you can never give it up. You have to keep doing it, hanging in there and finding what works. The passion is what will drive you to do your best, and doing your best is what will ultimately make your pursuit a successful one. I'm convinced that money follows passion. It's almost as if it seeks it out.

But it takes something else, too, as I mentioned above. Maryann and I worked our asses off. Seven days a week, twelve hours a day. Sometimes more. Often, we'd try to break away late in the afternoon and come home for an early dinner, but one of the employees would call us at home to let us know the shop was suddenly swamped and they needed our help. Some nights we'd close up at 10:00, only to have a few more customers straggle in, and we'd stay open even longer, not wanting to disappoint them. Most nights we'd just fall into bed.

Here's something that happens when you combine passion with hard work: breaks always come your way, if not right away, soon. You start finding luck. But it's not really luck; it's just the energy you're putting forth into the universe coming back to you. Maybe it's a karmic thing, who knows? All I know is that eventually a Paul Seegott comes along. Or a Mike Belkin. Or a Mayor Thomas Brick. Or in my case, all three. When people see you working so hard, they want to help, they want to be a part of it in some way. I know that these three gentlemen must have seen something in me that made them want to give me a boost. No doubt they saw something of their younger selves, back when they were just starting out, working hard, working passionately.

Interestingly enough, looking back, I can see that my dad was that way, always willing to help younger people just beginning their careers, and that explains the line of people at his wake, telling me how much he had meant to them. He'd seen himself in those people, and he had wanted them to succeed. Dad gave back, just like my three angels did

The customers gave back, too. They noticed the hard work and the passion. They saw how much effort and energy and love we were putting into the shop and they rewarded us with loyalty. They wanted to see us succeed. Customers appreciate effort. They notice it when you care, when you *really* care. If your customers want to see you succeed, then you've got the game won.

The employees picked up on the energy as well. I didn't keep anybody around who didn't get the concept of Dave's, and I could spot such an employee pretty quickly. Enthusiasm is a hard thing to fake for very long. If you worked for us, you had to understand, appreciate, and project the vibe. Above all else, Dave's was a fun place, and if you couldn't convey fun, you couldn't work for me.

And so the secret is a surprisingly simple one: passion and hard work open all the doors. I imagine it's the same in any pursuit. Do what you love, love what you do, work like hell, and never, ever give up.

Chapter 15

Highs and Lows

In 2023, I revisited the idea of producing my play "Voices." It had been sitting for years, and I decided to try to find an investor.

The play is important to me. Psychological disorders and the shame that's associated with them are issues that are near and dear to me. Bipolar disorder in particular is an illness that most people don't understand. Characterized by dramatic mood swings that run from manic episodes of elation, great creativity, or high energy to depressive episodes of sadness, anxiety, or feelings of hopelessness, bipolar is surprisingly common. How common? In the United States, approximately 6 million people are affected every year.

I didn't know this until I started writing this book. In fact, I didn't want to talk at all about my bipolar condition, but my editor told me how common bipolar is, and he also let me know that a lot of famous peo-

ple have it. Elvis Presley was bipolar. So are Catherine
Zeta-Jones, Linda Hamilton, Jane Pauley, Jean-Claude
Van Damm, Carrie Fisher, Mariah Carey, Brian Wil-
son, Buzz Aldrin, Francis Ford Coppola, Richard Drey-
fuss, Sting, Ted Turner, and Mel Gibson. Frank Sinatra
had bipolar disorder, as did Robin Williams. So did
Jimi Hendrix and Kurt Cobain. Virginia Woolf, Win-
ston Churchill, Theodore Roosevelt, Ernest Heming-
way, Vincent Van Gogh, and Ludwig Van Beethoven are
all believed to have suffered from manic mood swings
indicative of bipolar disorder.

What's interesting is that besides having bipolar disorder, all these people have something else in common:
high levels of creativity. I'm not suggesting that they
would not have been creative without their bipolar ten-
dencies, but there's no question that their upswings led
them to creative heights they may not have otherwise
reached. I look back at my own life and see the thread
of creativity that runs through it, from theater to rock
and roll to business. Dave's Cosmic Subs became much
more than a sandwich shop. Subway (with all due respect) is a sandwich shop. Jimmy John's (again, with
respect) is a sandwich shop. Dave's is an *idea*. A concept.
A wonderfully creative notion that I'm not sure would

have been possible without the passion that came by way of the good side of my bipolar.

I don't want to downplay the effects of the disorder. The bad side—the lows—are paralyzing. And if you're struggling with bipolar disorder, I recommend getting help. Don't suffer alone. Bipolar disorder is chronic but it can be controlled through therapy and medication.

In the meantime, keep an eye out for "Voices." I'm still looking for the right investor. Hopefully soon, it'll be coming to a stage near you.

In the end analysis, everyone in the world suffers highs and lows. Those of us with bipolar feel them more dramatically. Is this necessarily bad? A.J. Mendez, author, screenwriter, and retired professional female wrestler, puts it like this: "I could walk through fire if it meant making my dreams come true. That is the gift being bipolar gave me. It blessed me with a lofty imagination, an iron will, and an unbreakable belief in the impossible."

Recently, I put it another way. A friend of mine asked me about my bipolar disorder and I told him I would never trade it for normalcy. "I'd rather be fucked up and creative," I said.

Normalcy has never been for me. Give me passion. Give me creativity. Give me imagination and inspiration.

And, of course, give me rock and roll!

Acknowledgments

Special thanks to my loving parents for always believing in me.

My gratitude also to Chagrin Falls mayor Thomas Brick, and my dear friends and mentors, Mike Belkin and Paul Seegot.

Thanks to my dear friend and mentor, Jerry Payne, for his tremendous help in finishing this book.

And much appreciation to the thousands of people who became our beloved and valued customers and fans. Thank you all.

"What once was will never be again."

Francine and Charles Lombardy—Mom & Dad.

American Seaway Foods, Inc. That's Dad in the back, smoking.

The Beatles on the Ed Sullivan Show.
This changed everything for me.

My high school band—"The Collection."

Playing at the 1967 Spring dance.

Uncle Lester (the original angel) & Aunt Marie.

Jester Dinner Playhouse
presents
DAVID LOMBARDY
appearing as   in
El Gallo   'The Fantasticks'
Directed by John Draman

. . . sexy charm . . . terrific voice . . . makes the bandit a dashing figure."
—SIGRID MACY
The Ledger

"Handsome and lithe . . . rich, resonant singing adds great appeal to his poised characterization."
—LOIS DEAN
Star News

Jester Dinner Playhouse
525 Honolulu Blvd., Montrose
Fri., Sat., Sun.,
through Nov. 16   Res. **249-5071**

Starring in "The Fantasticks."

Dining And Entertainment.

Players To Stage 'Picnic'

The La Canada Players invite one and all to join them for a "Picnic" beginning March 13. This William Inge summer romance is a tale of young love and old passion and will feature David Lombardy as the bustling drifter, Hal.

David was seen in the last Players production, Agatha Christie's "The Hollow" as both the victim and a policeman (yes, that was him under Sgt. Penny's moustache). His diverse talents have taken him for a ride on "A Streetcar Named Desire" where he was seen as Stanley, and to the slums of "West Side Story" singing his heart out as the ill-fated Tony.

He was seen locally at the Jester Dinner Playhouse in Montrose as the sly El Gallo in the musical "The Fantasticks," and at the Jester Playhouse in Pasadena as the Prince in "The Unsinkable Molly Brown."

Make your plans now to join the Players for a "Picnic" under the direction of Glendale resident Patrick McMinn, seen in Players productions of "California Suite" and "Twelfth Night."

The Players "Picnic" begins March 13 and continues to April 4. Curtain time is 8:15 p.m. Fridays and Saturdays at The Oak Grove Auditorium, 140 Foothill Blvd., La Canada. General admission is $3.50 with senior citizens and students under age twelve being only $1.50. For information phone 790-1565 or 790-1334.

YOUNG LOVE has a stolen moment of romance in the La Canada Players production of William Inge's "Picnic." David Lombardy and Jo Ann Robinson are seen as the drifter and the young innocent from March 13 to April 4. Curtain is 8:15 p.m. Fridays and Saturdays at the Oak Grove Auditorium, 140 Foothill Blvd., La Canada. For information phone 790-1565 or 790-1334.

The lead in "Picnic."

alan presberg Productions
cordially invites you and your guest
to experience straight ahead rock'n'roll;

ANTHEM

Thursday, June 2, 1977

at

JTARWOOD

Crescent Heights & Santa Monica Blvd.
Hollywood

Two shows nightly 8:45 & 11:30
This invitation will admit you and your guest

RSVP 763-5212
(your name will be there anyways)

production and management
alan presberg
763-5212

representation
danny medina
273-5600

ANTHEM.
Our debut at the famous Starwood.

ANTHEM became Foreplay

On stage with Foreplay, doing what I did best.

Maryann and me.

In San Francisco

The original! *(Lynn Ischay/The Plain Dealer)*
(Historical picture)

Me out front. *(Thomas Ondrey/The Plain Dealer)*
(Historical picture)

Mike Belkin, one of my angels,
and the brains behind the free sub giveaway idea.

The Belkin Wall
(Historical picture)

I HAD A DREAM. YOU MADE IT A
REALITY. THANKS, CLEVELAND!!
ALWAYS, COSMIC DAVE

Lined up in the rain. *(Historical picture)*

Mayor Thomas Brick, another angel.
He saved the shop when the town wanted
to shut it down.

Paul Seegot with his wife Betsy. Paul, yet another angel, provided not only the space, but the encouragement we needed.

The interior.
(Historical picture)

(Historical picture)

Can't you feel the vibe?

(Historical picture)

174

We always got great publicity.

The counter. *(Lynn Ischay/The Plain Dealer)*
(Historical picture)

(Historical picture)

Me with Jimi and John. *(Lynn Ischay/ The Plain Dealer)*
(Historical picture)

176

With my secret sauce. *(Lynn Ischay/The Plain Dealer)*
(Historical picture)

Dave's Magic Bus
(Historical picture)

Brandon, our firstborn

Brandon working the counter. *(Lynn Ischay/The Plain Dealer)*
(Historical picture)

Rachael, our little cheerleader.

All grown up.

Love to all our fans in the Cosmic Nation.
—Dave and Maryanne

Cosmic Dave's legacy: The Original Dave's Cosmic Sauce!